D1371689

Old-

CHICAGO

Library of Congress Cataloging-in-Publication Data

Dailey, Pat
    Favorite old-fashioned desserts / Pat Dailey.
       p.   cm.
    Includes index.
    ISBN 0-8092-4092-8 (pbk.)
    1. Desserts.   I. Title.
TX773.D2   1991
641.8'6—dc20
                                  91-17997
                                      CIP

Published by Contemporary Books, Inc.
180 North Michigan Avenue, Chicago, Illinois 60601
Manufactured in the United States of America
International Standard Book Number: 0-8092-4092-0

For reasons that escape me entirely, this book is fondly dedicated to the third place and those who join me there.

Contents

Introduction

Just what is a "favorite old-fashioned" dessert? Is it a slice of Mom's apple pie, a big, moist, chewy brownie, a triple-scoop banana split? Or is it an ice cream cone eaten on a hot summer afternoon, a gooey slice of devil's food cake, or a chocolate chip cookie? The answer, of course, is any and all of the above. The roster of America's favorite old-fashioned desserts has as many entries as there are people who populate this vast and colorful land. And the list continues to grow and evolve just as the interest in regional American cooking does.

There is a certain core group of desserts that have a long history of being favorites of the American table. Indian pudding, for example, a delicious mixture of cornmeal, milk, and molasses has been around since colonial times and is most likely the oldest dessert to have the honor of being American. Some desserts heartily embrace our nation's ethnic diversity. America is a melting pot where cultures have mixed and mingled for decades, and out of this has come a wonderful legacy of foods, ensuring that an old-fashioned German fruit kuchen can be as much a favorite as old-fashioned apple pie.

Other desserts, such as persimmon pudding or pecan pie, are labeled old-fashioned because their basic ingredients are native to America and have long been used as foodstuffs. And still others get the distinction of being favorites because they have been so enthusiastically embraced by a populace that loves its sweet stuff. Anything and everything chocolate falls into this category, as well as such delights as crème brulée and a cheesecake made with Irish liqueur.

Clearly the world of desserts is very large, very sweet, and absolutely wonderful. So where to begin and where to end? I thought of all the desserts I have turned to over the years, the ones that didn't bow to faddishness or trends. These are the kinds of desserts that you'll find within these pages. Some, like a luscious fruit cobbler and a double-rich cheesecake, are stridently traditional because, frankly, they couldn't be improved. Others are the result of old standbys coming face to face with modern tastes and American ingenuity. You might find subtle twists in the flavorings or a slight divergence from traditional ingredients that add new sparkle and shine to long-standing favorites.

The desserts you will find here are easy to make. For the most part, none of the recipes has a long and complicated list of steps. Quantum physics is hard. Life itself is hard. Desserts should be easy.

Health concerns hover around us, threatening to dull the pleasures of the table, especially desserts. Some will argue that desserts are fattening, but they needn't be. Desserts and a balanced diet are not mutually exclusive. You can, it seems, with exercise and a sensible regimen, have your cake and eat it too.

Moderation tempered with some good common sense allows for occasional indulgences, whether it be eggs for breakfast, cheese sandwiches for lunch, or a grilled steak for dinner. Excess, in the form of a double slice of pie or a rich dessert every day and twice on Sunday, can be a problem. But so can abstinence. Life is meant to be enjoyed and if that involves a special dessert now and then, so be it.

Desserts fit into a larger scheme of life than just the dinner table. For those who love them, they are important for the pleasure they bring. I like desserts because they make people happy. They're the smile at the end of a meal, the sweet interlude during the day, the surreptitious treat that smacks of pure indulgence. In these hustle-and-bustle times, they're more welcome than ever.

But enough chattering. On to the good stuff.

1
Equipment

All cooks have their own *batterie de cuisine*—or equipment that makes up their kitchen. Certain items are practically indispensable. Imagine a kitchen without a vegetable peeler, for instance, or a toaster. What other more specialized items you need depends on what type of cooking you do. For making desserts, certain pieces of basic kitchen equipment are essential while others are just nice to have.

For generations of cooks, *electric mixers* were the workhorses of the kitchen, called into action for all manner of chores, from making cakes to cookies to pie doughs. They are still as capable of performing these tasks as they ever were, although they have been displaced somewhat by food processors.

Both mixers and processors have their own merits and both have a well-deserved place in making desserts. Mixers are still indispensable for mixing certain cake batters and for beating egg whites to a voluminous mountain of froth.

Food processors perform many of the more mundane kitchen chores—shredding, chopping, and slicing, for example—quite easily and quickly. They are very useful for mixing pie crusts, crumb toppings, cookie doughs, cheesecakes, and frostings. Many cake batters can be mixed in the processor as well.

The *microwave oven*, now standard equipment in almost all kitchens, is very useful for a number of things, from softening butter and melting chocolate to making certain sauces and fillings. Whenever instructions are given in this book for using a microwave oven, a more conventional method can be used—the end results will be the same.

A few of the recipes here include cooking times in the microwave oven. These times were based on the use of a 650- to 700-watt oven. If your microwave oven has a lower wattage, adjust the timing accordingly. Even in the best of circumstances, these times are meant to be guidelines, not dictates.

A certain array of *baking pans* are stock items in most kitchens; others are somewhat more specialized. You might find that you don't have all of the pans called for within these pages. If the recipe really intrigues you, you'll probably be inclined to seek out and buy the pan. For the most part, baking pans aren't as expensive as stove-top cookware; so the investment won't be too large—and it will pay off rather sweetly.

Accurate *measuring equipment* just may be the most important tools in a kitchen. Dessert making can be an exact science. Adding the wrong measurement of certain key ingredients can spell doom and disaster. Since there aren't any government standards for measuring spoons and cups, buy good-quality, recognized brands. Foley makes excellent measuring cups and spoons.

There are two types of measuring cups: those used for measuring liquids and those used for measuring dry ingredients. A cup is a cup, so both types measure the same amounts. Certain design features, however, make each one more appropriate for its intended use. Liquid measuring cups are usually made of glass, have a pouring spout, and have a margin at the top so the liquid doesn't spill over the rim. Dry measuring cups are usually made of plastic or metal and are flush across the top. The gradations go right to the top on dry measuring cups. They are usually sold in nesting sets that measure ¼ cup, ⅓ cup, ½ cup, and 1 cup.

An *oven thermometer* is absolutely essential in dessert making because oven temperatures can vary significantly from what the oven's gauge indicates. A good mercury thermometer will tell exactly what the temperature is inside the oven so that your baking temperatures will be precise. Don't buy a spring-type thermometer—they aren't very accurate. A mercury oven thermometer costs only ten to twelve dollars. It will more than pay for itself over time.

Thermometers should be tested occasionally to see if they are still registering precise readings. To test a thermometer, immerse it in boiling water. It should read 212°F.

2
Techniques

For all the mystique surrounding them, cooking and baking involve nothing more than following a given list of instructions. There are no mystical secrets to becoming a good or even a great cook. It is just a matter of following instructions and practicing. Repetitive attempts make things easier and quicker. Most likely, the end results will be better as well.

Here are a few techniques to learn that are basic to baking and dessert making—you may already know some of them. They are not difficult nor do they require highly developed skills. As with many things, it may be awkward at first to utilize them, but each successive endeavor gets easier and gives markedly improved results. In time you may even discover your own tricks.

Melting Chocolate

There are two primary ways to melt chocolate—on the top of the stove or in the microwave oven. Whichever method you choose, a great deal of care must be taken to ensure that the chocolate does not burn. Burned chocolate not only tastes bitter but has a coarse, grainy texture. Ideally, chocolate should not be heated above 120°F, which could be described as warm rather than hot.

Chocolate should be cut into small pieces so it will melt more quickly and evenly. This is easily done by hand, although if you have a large amount to cut, you might want to chop it in a food processor.

The easiest way to melt chocolate is in the microwave oven. To do so, put the chocolate in a microwave-safe bowl. Microwave it, uncovered, using 50 percent power. Six ounces of chocolate will usually melt in about 3 minutes at 50 percent power. The time it takes chocolate to melt in the microwave oven will depend on the amount of chocolate you're melting and the wattage of your oven, so keep careful watch over it. Like many foods heated in the microwave oven, chocolate heats from the inside out, so it is important to stir it several times during the cooking time.

If other ingredients such as butter or sugar are melted with the chocolate, the timing will be quite a bit different. Experience will be your best guide but, remember, it is always better to err on the conservative side. Begin with 1 minute increments of time, stirring each minute. Toward the end, heat in shorter increments to avoid overheating the chocolate.

You can also melt chocolate in a double boiler on the stove. Chop the chocolate first, and then put it in the top of a double boiler placed over very gently simmering water. The upper pan that holds the chocolate should not rest in the water. Stir the chocolate occasionally and remove it from the heat as soon as the chocolate is smooth.

Many recipes call for chocolate to be melted with water. Much has been made of the fact that if a single drop of water gets into chocolate, it will be ruined. This is true, to some extent. A small amount of water—a drop or two—will play havoc with pure chocolate, causing it to seize up and become tight. A greater amount of water (or other liquid such as coffee), however, creates no problem.

Sifting Flour

Many years ago, sifting flour was an absolute necessity because flour was milled more coarsely and less consistently than it is today. Now sifting is often unnecessary—but there are still times when it is required.

When a recipe calls for "1 cup sifted flour," the flour must be sifted before it is measured because sifted flour weighs less than unsifted flour.

On the other hand, if the recipe says "1 cup flour, sifted" this means the flour is to be sifted after it has been measured. This will apply primarily to cake flour. Because cake flour tends to lump, it should always be sifted before it is used. In the recipes in this book, cake flour is measured first, and then sifted.

Sifting is usually done with a flour sifter. If you don't have one, however, you can press the flour through a fine-mesh strainer.

Toasting Nuts

Almost without exception, I prefer to toast nuts before using them in a recipe.

Toasting crisps the nuts and improves their texture, and it deepens and enhances their flavor.

To toast nuts, spread them on a baking sheet. Bake them at 400°F in a preheated oven until they deepen in color and become aromatic. Baking time varies depending on the type and size of nut and the oven temperature. Smaller nuts, such as pine nuts, may begin to toast after 5 to 7 minutes. Larger ones may take 10 to 12 minutes. In any event, they should be closely watched, especially toward the end of the baking. After they begin to toast, they are just a few seconds away from burning.

If you are preheating the oven for a recipe, the nuts can be toasted at that same temperature. Simply adjust the timing up or down to compensate for the change in temperature.

Preparing Pans

There are few things more disheartening than baking a prefect-looking cake only to have it stick to the pan. This situation can be avoided by taking care to prepare the pans properly. Even if you use nonstick baking pans, they should be greased when greasing is specified in the recipe.

Several types of fat are appropriate for greasing baking pans. Softened butter and solid vegetable shortening, such as Crisco, are my two favorite choices. Both coat the surface of a pan thickly and evenly, and both have very good release properties. To apply them, I use a wadded paper towel or a piece of waxed paper. Nonstick cooking sprays are easy to use, and I use them when I'm in a hurry.

Recipes often call for the baking pan to be dusted with flour after it has been greased. The flour works in tandem with the grease to form a releasable bond for certain cakes that may be otherwise difficult to remove from the pan. Another advantage of flouring a pan is this: Flour won't stick to a surface that hasn't been greased, so you'll be able to see if the pan isn't completely greased.

All-purpose flour works just fine for flouring pans. If you use cake flour, it should be sifted first or there will be lumps. To dust a pan, toss a handful of flour into the greased pan and tilt the pan so the flour coats the entire inside surface. Once you're satisfied that it is fully coated with a thin film of flour, hold the pan upside down over the sink and gently tap it several times so the excess flour falls out. If excess flour is left in the pan, the cake will have a gloppy, white coating of flour when it comes out of the pan.

Occasionally a recipe will require that a pan be lined with waxed paper or parchment paper. Unless the recipe states otherwise, this refers just to the bottom of the pan, not the sides. To prepare the paper, trace an outline of the pan bottom on the paper, cut it out, and trim it if necessary. For the best results, the paper should fit neatly right into the bottom of the pan.

Grating Citrus Zest

When removing the zest from citrus fruit, remove only the very thin outer layer that is colored. Immediately underneath the colored zest is a thick layer of spongy white pith. The pith tastes bitter and even the smallest amount can give an unpleasant edge to a recipe.

For me, grating zest was always more difficult than it seemed it should be. Many hand graters either mince it so fine that the zest never really falls from the grater or so coarse that it is unpleasant in the finished recipe. Citrus zesters leave the zest in pretty big pieces. A food processor works fairly well but only if the zest is minced with sugar or flour. By itself, there isn't enough in the bowl to get it moving around the blade. Perseverance finally paid off for me, however, and I have found a four-sided grater that does a terrific job. That's my answer. Maybe you're lucky and have had a terrific grater all along. But if you're not satisfied, try a new grater.

Beating Egg Whites

The purpose of beating egg whites is to incorporate air into them. The trapped bubbles of air then serve either as leavening, or they lighten the recipe in which they are used.

Begin by separating the eggs. Eggs are easier to separate when they are taken right from the refrigerator because the white is then firmer. I prefer to crack the egg and pour it into my hand, which I have placed over a cup to catch the egg white. As the fingers are spread open ever so slightly, the white slips through, leaving the yolk intact. It helps facilitate the separation process if you pass the yolk back and forth between your hands. Other cooks crack the egg in half and then pour the egg yolk back and forth between the two halves of the shell. It has been my experience that the chances of puncturing the yolk are much greater with this method because the yolk slides back and forth over the jagged shell.

Eggs must be beaten in a bowl that is absolutely clean. Even the smallest smidgen of grease will keep egg whites from attaining their fullest volume. Select a bowl that is quite large since the whites will expand greatly as they are beaten.

Begin beating the egg whites with an electric mixer on low speed. When they are frothy, add a small amount of cream of tartar, which helps to stabilize the whites. If the recipe you are using doesn't specify the use of cream of tartar—or doesn't specify how much to use—add ¼ teaspoon for every 4 egg whites. Once the cream of tartar has been added, increase the mixer speed to high. Continue beating until the whites hold their shape but are still creamy and soft. If the bowl is held upside down, the whites should remain firmly in place. (Trying this takes a bit of confidence the first time.) Egg whites should not be beaten to the point at which they become dry and separate when they are lifted from the bowl with a spoon.

In some recipes, sugar is added to the egg whites as they are being beaten. When sugar is added, the whites should be beaten longer than when they are beaten alone. Add the sugar 1 tablespoon or so at a time, beating thoroughly between each addition. When fully beaten, whites with sugar will be thick, glossy, and creamy smooth.

3
Ingredients
❊⊛❊

Baking is a special endeavor that must be done with care. But no matter how skillful you are in techniques, the result will be only as good as the ingredients that go into the recipe. Don't cut corners. Buy the best ingredients, make sure they're fresh, and handle them properly.

Butter

I always use unsalted butter for baking. Unsalted butter has a pure taste that is infinitely more palatable than salted butter. Its taste is especially noticeable in delicate baked goods.

You might question the logic in calling for unsalted butter and then adding salt to a recipe. When the butter manufacturer adds salt, I have no control over the amount. When I use unsalted butter and couple it with a small amount of salt, however, I know exactly how much salt to add to achieve the balance of taste I'm looking for.

Unsalted butter is more perishable than salted butter. For this reason, your market may keep it in the freezer section rather than in the dairy case. At home, it's a good idea to store all but a small supply in the freezer.

You will often see "softened" butter called for in recipes. Softened butter is simply butter that can be smeared easily. You should be able to press it with the back of a spoon and have it give without any pressure. It should not, however, be softened to the point that it has liquefied at all.

Some cooks will be tempted to use margarine, whether it be for reasons of health, habit, or economy. In many instances, it will work just fine, but I make no guarantees. A pound cake, for instance, simply isn't worth making if it doesn't have the taste of real, honest-to-goodness butter. But if you must use margarine, by all means use unsalted margarine.

Eggs

All of these recipes require USDA large eggs. For the best results, they should be at room temperature (although they should not be left out of the refrigerator longer than 30 to 45 minutes). Cold eggs added to a creamed butter/sugar mixture will cause it to solidify.

Up until recently, raw eggs were used without any trepidation. Now, with an increase in the cases of salmonella food poisoning stemming from raw shell eggs, people are questioning whether using raw eggs is safe. To use them or not is a decision you must make for yourself. Very few recipes in this book call for raw eggs.

Flour

Unbleached all-purpose flour is an excellent product; however, it is not necessarily the best choice in all cases. There are some recipes that all-purpose flour is well suited for, but for many desserts, cake flour is far superior.

Cake flour is milled from a softer wheat than all-purpose flour and thus has less protein. What this all boils down to for the baker is that cakes made with cake flour have a softer texture, which in most cakes is a decided asset.

Cake flour tends to lump and cake together more than all-purpose flour. For this reason it must be sifted before it is added to batters. However, the *cake flour measurements called for are always for flour that is not yet sifted.* A cup of sifted flour is not the same as a cup of unsifted flour. Cake flour weighs 4 ounces per cup before sifting and about 3¼ ounces after sifting, which is a pretty significant difference—certainly enough to affect the outcome of your baked goods.

To measure flour, I use the 3-S method—stir, scoop, and sweep. First stir or fluff the flour up with a fork, and then, using a dry measuring cup, scoop up the flour. (Note: if the recipe calls for ¾ cup of flour, the measure will be more precise if you use a ½ cup measure and a ¼ cup measure rather than trying to gauge ¾ of a 1-cup measure.) Then take the flat edge of a knife and sweep off the mounded flour so that the flour is exactly level with the top rim of the measuring cup.

Sugar and Other Sweeteners

Unless another type is specified in the ingredients list, sugar refers to granulated white sugar.

When measuring light or dark brown sugar, pack it tightly, but not forcefully, into a cup. Do not substitute granulated brown sugar in these recipes.

Confectioners' sugar is also known as powdered sugar. Like cake flour, it has a tendency to lump. Measure it first, and then sift or strain it before using it.

When maple syrup is called for, ideally pure maple syrup should be used. Costly as it is, it is well worth it. Maple-flavored pancake syrup, however, can be used with acceptable results.

Baking Powder

Almost without exception, all baking powders on the market are double acting. Most cans have an expiration date stamped on the bottom. Make sure yours is still fresh. It is also a good idea to shake the can before using it because some of the particles are heavier than others and tend to settle at the bottom of the can.

Baking Soda

Baking soda has a tendency to lump. When you measure it, press out any lumps, especially if it is not to be sifted with the flour before it is added to a batter.

Dairy Products

Milk always refers to whole milk, sour cream to dairy sour cream and not light sour cream or sour half-and-half. Whipping cream is called heavy cream in some regions of the country. Cream labeled with either designation can be used. Yogurt refers to low-fat yogurt. Soured milk, fresh milk that has purposely been soured with a small amount of vinegar, can be used in place of buttermilk. (Milk that has soured through age should not be used because it may have other bacteria that are not safe to consume.) To sour milk, put 1 tablespoon of distilled white or cider vinegar into a 1-cup measuring cup. Add milk to bring the level to 1 cup. Let it stand about 5 minutes before using it.

A note on measuring yogurt and sour cream. Since these products are semisolid, they are sold by weight rather than by fluid ounces. Thus an 8-ounce carton of yogurt has on its container markings a reference to its weight, not its cup measurement. Eight ounces of yogurt measure only ¾ cup. Eight ounces of sour cream measure slightly less than a cup. Always measure these ingredients in a measuring cup instead of relying on the markings on the containers.

Chocolate

The brands of chocolate sold in supermarkets will turn out a perfectly acceptable product. There are some premium brands, however (Ghirardelli, Maillard, and Valhrona, to name a few), that aren't too difficult to track down that will make the finished product even better. Often they are no more expensive than the supermarket brands.

There are no strict guidelines for the labeling of chocolate. Thus one manufacturer's semisweet chocolate may be as sweet as another's sweet chocolate.

Bitter or unsweetened chocolate has had no sugar added to it at all. Do not confuse bitter chocolate with bittersweet chocolate. Bittersweet chocolate has had some sugar added and is more akin to semisweet chocolate. Bittersweet tends to be French terminology, but you will see it on products sold in the States. Sweet chocolate is usually the sweetest of the chocolates used for baking. Milk chocolate—with the most sugar, as well as with additional milk solids added—should not be used for cooking unless it is specified in the recipe.

Nuts

Nuts should always be fresh. Because they contain oil, nuts can become rancid over time. For prolonged storage, keep them in the freezer.

Almost without exception, I prefer to toast nuts before using them in a recipe. Toasting crisps the nuts and improves their texture, and it deepens and enhances their flavor. (See Index for reference on how to toast nuts.)

Vanilla

Always use pure vanilla extract, not imitation vanilla.

4
Cakes and Cheesecakes

Angel Food Cake

Perfect Golden Butter Cake

Cream Cheese Pound Cake

Fe Fi Fo Rum Cake

Chocolate Fudge Brownie Cake

Deep-Dark Fudge Cake

Flourless Chocolate Cake

German Chocolate Cake

Whoopie Pies

Almond Butter Cream Cake with Tart Cherries

Annie Apple Cake

Banana Cake Roll

Lemon Velvet Cake

Peaches and Cream Cake

Spicy Lemon Gingerbread

Strawberry Shortcake

Forty-Karat Carrot Cake

Flavors of Christmas Cake

Boston Cream Pie

Creamy Cheesecake

Peter, Peter Pumpkin Cheesecake

Dailey's Irish Cream Cheesecake

Angel Food Cake

Makes 1 10-inch cake
10 to 12 servings

Snowy white and light as a feather, Angel Food Cake is guaranteed to elicit appreciative oohs and aahs whenever it is served. Angel Food Cake has several notable traits—it has absolutely no fat and no cholesterol and is relatively low in calories (at least until you pile on the whipped cream).

Making a big, beautiful angel food cake from scratch is not all that difficult, despite what you may have been led to believe. And the heavenly rewards are more than worth the effort. A dusting of confectioners' sugar and it's ready for serving, although you can add a simple glaze, if that's your preference. Fresh seasonal fruit is a sensational accompaniment.

1½ cups superfine sugar (see Note)
¾ cup plus 2 tablespoons cake flour
14 large egg whites
1 teaspoon cream of tartar
1 teaspoon pure vanilla extract
Drop almond extract

Place a rack in the center of the oven and preheat the oven to 350°F. Have an ungreased 10-inch tube pan ready.

Sift together ¾ cup of the sugar and all of the flour 3 times.

Put the egg whites in a 5-quart bowl. Beat with an electric mixer on low speed until they are foamy. Add the cream of tartar, vanilla, and almond extract and increase the mixer speed to high. Beating constantly as you do so, add the remaining ¾ cup of sugar a little at a time, mixing thoroughly between each addition. When all of the sugar has been added, the whites should be thick, glossy, and voluminous.

Sift half of the flour mixture over the whites and fold it in gently, using a flat whisk if you have one or else a slotted skimmer or a large rubber spatula. Make sure to mix all the way to the bottom of the bowl, but be gentle so the whites do not deflate. Repeat with the remaining flour mixture. Transfer the batter to the pan and cut through it in several places with a knife to break up any air pockets. Smooth the surface with a rubber spatula.

Bake until the cake is golden and set, 32 to 38 minutes. Do not overbake it or the cake will begin to deflate. Invert the pan, using the neck of a bottle if the pan doesn't have little "feet" to raise it from the counter. Let the cake cool completely in the upside-down position. Loosen it from the side of the pan with a small knife and invert it onto a serving plate.

Note: If you don't have superfine sugar, simply process granulated sugar in a food processor with the metal blade for 1 or 2 minutes. Measure the sugar after it has been processed.

Perfect Golden Butter Cake

Makes 1 9-inch layer cake
10 servings

One of the most neglected and underrated cakes is the old-fashioned yellow cake. Simple in its charms, this cake can be dressed up with a wide variety of fillings and toppings. This is the best version I have, tender and light as a feather.

My choice for a frosting is the glossy, satiny Milk Chocolate Frosting (see Index). You might, as I occasionally do, pair this cake with a maple buttercream or maybe a caramel, coffee, or brown-butter frosting instead.

4 large eggs
½ cup solid vegetable shortening
1 stick unsalted butter, softened
1 cup granulated sugar
1¼ cups cake flour
2 teaspoons baking powder
½ cup whole milk
1 teaspoon pure vanilla extract
¼ teaspoon cream of tartar
Milk Chocolate Frosting (see Index) or
 frosting of your choice

Heat the oven to 350°F. Butter two 9-inch round layer cake pans. Separate the yolks and whites of three of the eggs. Leave the fourth egg whole.

Cream the shortening, butter, and sugar with an electric mixer on high speed for 2 minutes, until the mixture is light and fluffy. Add the whole egg and 3 egg yolks and mix 2 minutes longer. Sift the cake flour with the baking powder; add the vanilla to the milk; add the flour mixture alternately with the milk and vanilla, mixing lightly.

In a clean bowl with clean beaters, beat the egg whites until they are foamy. Add the cream of tartar and mix on high speed until they hold soft peaks. Gently fold the whites into the batter.

Divide the batter between the prepared pans. Bake until a toothpick inserted in the center comes out clean, 22 to 25 minutes. Let the cakes cool in the pan for 5 minutes and then turn them out onto a wire rack to cool completely. Fill and frost as desired.

Cream Cheese Pound Cake

Makes 1 10-inch cake
10 to 12 servings

Simplicity does have its virtues, as this old-fashioned cake tasting of butter and vanilla so amply attests. It is a large cake, but then it ought to be—it has a way of disappearing very quickly. It can be glazed with a simple confectioners' sugar glaze (see recipe below) or dusted with confectioners' sugar just before it's served. Fresh fruit is a perfect accompaniment. If there is any cake left over, toast some slices for a tea-time treat.

CAKE
3 cups cake flour
¼ teaspoon salt
3 sticks unsalted butter, softened
1 package (8 ounces) cream cheese,
  softened
4 cups (1 pound) confectioners' sugar
6 large eggs
Grated zest of 1 lemon
1 tablespoon bourbon
1 teaspoon pure vanilla extract

GLAZE
1 cup confectioners' sugar
1½ tablespoons unsalted butter, melted
1 tablespoon whole milk
1 teaspoon lemon juice
1 teaspoon pure vanilla extract
1 teaspoon bourbon

Heat the oven to 325°F. Generously butter a 10-inch tube pan. Dust the inside lightly with flour and tap out the excess. Sift the flour and salt together and set aside.

Beat the butter and cream cheese with an electric mixer until smooth. Add the sugar and mix on high speed 3 minutes. Add the eggs, one at a time, mixing well after each addition. Add the lemon zest, bourbon, and vanilla and mix well. Stop the mixer and add the flour and salt. Mix just until combined.

Transfer the batter to the prepared pan. Bake until a toothpick inserted in the center comes out clean, 80 to 90 minutes. Cool the cake in the pan 10 minutes and then gently loosen it from the sides of the pan with a small knife. Invert it onto a wire rack.

To make the glaze, combine all ingredients and mix until smooth. Spoon the glaze over the top of the warm cake, letting it drip down the sides.

Fe Fi Fo Rum Cake

Makes 1 loaf cake
8 servings

This is a light golden butter cake, flavored with ginger and very aggressively anointed with rum. It can be made with Amaretto, Grand Marnier, or Kahlua instead of rum, in which case you should leave out the ginger. If you prefer a less moist cake, halve the amount of syrup called for.

CAKE
1 stick unsalted butter, softened
1 cup granulated sugar
2 large eggs
¼ cup light rum
¼ cup buttermilk
1 teaspoon very finely minced
    crystallized ginger (this is usually 3
    pieces from a jar of ginger)
1¼ cups unbleached all-purpose flour
½ teaspoon baking powder
½ teaspoon baking soda
⅛ teaspoon salt

RUM SYRUP
½ cup light corn syrup
⅓ cup water
2½ tablespoons unsalted butter
⅓ cup light rum

Heat the oven to 350°F. Butter a 5- to 6-cup loaf pan and line the bottom with a sheet of parchment paper or waxed paper.

Cream the butter and sugar with an electric mixer on high speed until the mixture is light, 2 minutes. Add the eggs, one at a time, mixing well after each addition. Continue to mix for an additional minute. Stop the mixer and add the rum, buttermilk, and minced ginger; mix well. Stop the mixer again and add the flour, baking powder, baking soda, and salt. Mix on low speed just until combined.

Transfer the batter to the prepared pan. Bake until a toothpick inserted in the center comes out clean, about 45 minutes.

While the cake is baking, prepare the syrup. Combine the corn syrup, water, and butter in a small pan. Bring to a boil and cook until the butter is melted and the mixture is smooth. Remove from the heat and stir in the rum.

After the cake is baked, remove it from the oven and, with a long slender skewer or a toothpick, poke holes all over its top. Slowly pour some syrup over the cake, letting it drip down the sides of the cake. The cake can take only so much syrup at a time; it will be necessary to let it soak in for a few minutes, and then come back and add some more. Once all of the syrup has been added, loosen the cake from the sides of the pan with a small knife. Invert the cake onto a rack, shaking the pan if necessary to loosen the bottom. Turn the cake upright on the rack and let it cool completely. Wrap the cake tightly in plastic wrap and let it stand at least 6 hours or overnight before serving.

Chocolate Fudge Brownie Cake

Makes 1 9-inch cake
8 to 10 servings

This dense, cocoa-rich treat is quite similar to a flourless cake, although it does contain the tiniest bit of flour. The big difference between it and a flourless version is that this is ridiculously easy to make.

CAKE
8 ounces semisweet or bittersweet
  chocolate
2 sticks unsalted butter
1 cup granulated sugar
4 large eggs, lightly beaten
1 tablespoon pure vanilla extract
2 tablespoons cocoa powder
2 tablespoons unbleached all-purpose
  flour

TOPPING
2 tablespoons confectioners' sugar
1 tablespoon granulated sugar

Heat the oven to 325°F. Cut a circle of waxed paper to fit the bottom of a 9-inch springform pan. Butter the pan, add the paper, and butter the paper. Sprinkle the inside with flour or cocoa powder and tap out the excess.

Melt the chocolate with the butter and granulated sugar in a microwave oven or in the top of a double boiler over gently simmering water. Stir until smooth and cool slightly.

Whisk the eggs and vanilla into the chocolate mixture, and then stir in the cocoa and flour. Transfer the batter to the prepared pan. Wrap the bottom of the pan in aluminum foil so no water can get inside. Place the wrapped pan in a shallow roasting pan and add 1 inch of water to the bottom of the roasting pan. Bake until cake is set, about 70 minutes.

Remove the pan from the water bath and let it cool to room temperature. When cool, remove the sides from the pan. Loosen the cake from the bottom of the pan with a long metal spatula, and then invert it onto a cake plate and remove the bottom of the pan. Peel away the waxed paper. Refrigerate at least 2 hours or up to 2 days before serving.

At serving time, mix the two sugars together. Sift a heavy coating over the top of the cake.

Deep-Dark Fudge Cake

Makes 1 13″ × 9″ cake
12 servings

Can there ever really be enough recipes for chocolate cake? Probably not, and certainly this is not one too many when it is this easy to make. It is the simplest of the lot, just the kind of cake that will gladden the hearts of hurried or timid bakers. Given the chance to last, it will stay marvelously soft and fresh for a day or two. It is exceedingly rich and moist, with a soft, fine texture. The chocolate frosting is marvelously creamy, silky smooth, and light.

CAKE

4 ounces semisweet or bittersweet
   chocolate
¼ cup water (or coffee, if you like a
   mocha flavor)
6 tablespoons unsweetened cocoa
   powder
1½ cups cake flour
½ cup light brown sugar
½ cup granulated sugar
1½ teaspoons baking soda
¼ teaspoon baking powder
Pinch salt
2 sticks unsalted butter, softened
4 large eggs
¾ cup sour cream
2 teaspoons pure vanilla extract

MILK CHOCOLATE FROSTING

4 ounces semisweet or bittersweet
   chocolate
½ cup granulated sugar
1 cup whipping cream
1 stick unsalted butter, softened
2 teaspoons pure vanilla extract

Heat the oven to 350°F. Generously butter a 13″ × 9″ cake pan. Melt the chocolate with the water (or coffee) in the microwave oven or in a double boiler. Remove it from the heat and add the cocoa. Stir the mixture until smooth and then set it aside to cool until it is tepid.

Combine the flour, both sugars, baking soda, baking powder, and salt in the bowl of an electric mixer. Mix on low speed for 20 seconds or until the ingredients are well combined. Cut the butter into tablespoon-size pieces and add it to the dry ingredients. Mix on low speed until the butter is uniformly mixed in, about 30 seconds. At this point, the batter will not look smooth. Add the eggs, sour cream, vanilla, and chocolate mixture. Turn the mixer to high speed and mix 3 minutes.

Transfer the batter to the prepared pan, smoothing the surface with a rubber spatula. Bake until a toothpick inserted in the center comes out clean, 35 to 40 minutes. Cool completely before frosting.

For the frosting, cut the chocolate into small pieces and set it aside. Combine the sugar and cream in a medium-sized heavy saucepan and bring to a boil over high heat, stirring often. Starting from the time the mixture is at a rolling boil, cook 5 minutes. Remove from the heat and add the chocolate. Stir until smooth. Cut the butter into pieces and add it, stirring until smooth. Add the vanilla and mix well. Place the frosting in the refrigerator, watching carefully, and remove it when it is chilled and thickened, before it is solidly set.

Beat the frosting with an electric mixer until it lightens in color and is smooth and fluffy. Spread it over the cake.

Flourless Chocolate Cake

Makes 1 9-inch cake
10 to 12 servings

The mere mention of a flourless chocolate cake sends shivers of rapture through many a dessert lover. Dark, dense, rich, moist, and exceedingly chocolatey, it's a welcome remnant of the nouvelle cuisine era.

When properly made, a flourless chocolate cake looks for all the world like a cake gone wrong. The top cracks, the sides slope, and there's usually a crater in the middle. Oddly enough, these are all signs of success. Serve the cake in thin slices, either topped with a simple mound of whipped cream or atop a pool of Creamy Custard Sauce (see Index).

CAKE
8 ounces semisweet or bittersweet
  chocolate
1 stick unsalted butter
7 large eggs, separated
½ cup granulated sugar
3 tablespoons orange-flavored liqueur
  or brandy
1 teaspoon pure vanilla extract
¾ teaspoon cream of tartar

TOPPING
2 tablespoons confectioners' sugar
1 tablespoon granulated sugar
2 teaspoons unsweetened cocoa powder
Sweetened whipped cream or Creamy
  Custard Sauce (see Index) for garnish

Heat the oven to 250°F. Butter a 9-inch springform pan and dust the inside with unsweetened cocoa powder.

Melt the chocolate with the butter in a microwave oven or in the top of a double boiler. Remove from the heat and set aside.

Beat the egg yolks, ¼ cup granulated sugar, liqueur, and vanilla with an electric mixer on high speed until the mixture is light, 2 minutes. Add the chocolate mixture and mix thoroughly.

In a clean bowl with clean beaters, beat the egg whites on low speed until they are foamy. Add the cream of tartar and increase the speed to high. Beat until the whites hold soft peaks. Gradually add the remaining ¼ cup granulated sugar, mixing well after each addition. Gently but thoroughly fold the egg whites into the chocolate mixture.

Transfer batter to the prepared pan. Bake until the cake is set in the center, about 1½ hours. The top will have a crust and perhaps some large surface cracks— this is all right.

Place the pan on a wire rack and cool the cake completely. When it is cool, loosen it from the sides of the pan and then remove the sides. Transfer the cake to a serving plate.

At serving time, stir confectioners' sugar, granulated sugar, and cocoa together and sift it over the cake. Serve with whipped cream or custard sauce.

German Chocolate Cake

Makes 1 9-inch cake
10 to 12 servings

German chocolate cakes are wonderfully rich and gooey. If you haven't tried one lately, it might be time you did. They withstand the test of time and taste as good now as they ever did—maybe better.

This one is especially rich and moist. The exceptionally creamy topping is filled to capacity with toasted pecans and shredded coconut. Sour cream is used in place of whipping or heavy cream, which lends a pleasing tang that perfectly complements the sweetness of the cake.

CAKE
4 ounces sweet cooking chocolate, such
    as Ghirardelli dark sweet
½ cup water
2 cups cake flour
1¼ teaspoons baking soda
¼ teaspoon salt
1¾ cups granulated sugar
2 sticks unsalted butter, softened
4 large eggs
1 cup plain yogurt (see Note)
2 teaspoons pure vanilla extract

FILLING AND FROSTING
5 large egg yolks
1¼ cups sour cream
¾ cup granulated sugar
½ cup light brown sugar
4 tablespoons unsalted butter
1 teaspoon unsweetened cocoa powder
2⅔ cups (7-ounce package) sweetened
    flaked coconut
1½ cups toasted chopped pecans
2 teaspoons pure vanilla extract

Place a rack in the center of the oven and preheat the oven to 350°F. Butter three 9-inch round layer cake pans. Line the bottoms of the pans with circles of waxed paper and butter the paper.

Melt the chocolate with the water in a small pan or in the microwave oven. Cool slightly. Sift the flour, baking soda, and salt together and set aside.

Cream the granulated sugar and butter with an electric mixer on high speed until the mixture is smooth, light, and fluffy, 2 to 3 minutes. Add the eggs, one at a time, mixing well after each addition. Turn the mixer to low speed and add the yogurt, vanilla, and chocolate mixture. Mix well. Stop the mixer and add the dry ingredients. Blend just until the batter is smooth.

Divide the batter among the three pans. Bake until a toothpick inserted in the center comes out clean, 22 to 25 minutes. Cool the cake in the pans for 5 minutes and then loosen the layers from the sides of the pans. Invert the layers onto a wire rack. Cool the layers completely before filling.

To make the filling, whisk the egg yolks in a medium-sized heavy pan. Add the sour cream, both sugars, butter, and cocoa and cook over medium heat, stirring constantly, until the mixture thickens, 12 to 15 minutes. Remove from the heat and add the coconut, pecans, and vanilla. Cool completely.

To assemble the cake, place one layer on a serving plate. Spread it with a thin layer of filling. Repeat layering with the other two layers and then spread the remaining filling over the top and sides of the cake.

Note: Remember, an 8-ounce carton of yogurt equals only ¾ cup. You will therefore need 1⅓ cartons of yogurt. Drain off any liquid that has accumulated on top before you measure the yogurt.

Whoopie Pies

Makes about 20 pies

These big, saucer-shaped "pies" are a favorite old-fashioned treat in many areas of the country, and for good reason. Two chocolate cakes are sandwiched together with a filling of fluffy, pure-white frosting. If you wish, you may add an extra flavoring that suits your fancy to the filling, or forego the filling entirely and use ice cream instead. This recipe, by the way, is very much a part of Mennonite cooking. It is a delicious tradition to spread around.

CAKES
⅔ cup whole milk
2 teaspoons distilled white vinegar
½ cup solid vegetable shortening
1 cup granulated sugar
1 large egg
1 teaspoon pure vanilla extract
½ cup unsweetened cocoa powder
1 teaspoon baking soda
½ cup hot tap water
2 cups unbleached all-purpose flour
½ teaspoon salt

FILLING
3 cups confectioners' sugar
⅓ cup solid vegetable shortening
3 tablespoons whole milk
1 large egg white

Heat the oven to 350°F. Grease the baking sheet or sheets. Combine the milk and vinegar and let the mixture stand for 10 minutes.

Cream the shortening and granulated sugar with an electric mixer until it is light and fluffy. Add the egg and vanilla and mix thoroughly. Stop the mixer and add the cocoa. Slowly blend it in at low speed, and then add the milk mixture. Stir the baking soda into the hot water. Add it to the mixture, alternating it with the flour and salt. Let the batter stand at room temperature for 15 minutes.

Drop the batter by generous spoonfuls onto the prepared baking sheet or sheets, forming 2-inch rounds. Bake just until they are set, 7 to 9 minutes. Transfer them to a wire rack and cool completely before filling them.

For the filling, beat the confectioners' sugar, shortening, milk, and egg white with an electric mixer on high speed until they are light, fluffy, and shiny, 2 to 3 minutes.

Matching cakes by size and shape, sandwich two together with filling. Store them in an airtight container.

Almond Butter Cream Cake
with Tart Cherries

Makes 1 10-inch bundt cake
10 to 12 servings

This is a big, moist, butter-rich cake, enticingly flavored with almond paste and tart dried cherries. It slices thin, keeps well, and always pleases guests.

Dried red cherries are becoming more and more commonly available in food markets. They are intensely flavored little nuggets that infuse the cake with flecks of color and a lovely fruit flavor. Other dried fruits—apricots, cranberries, blueberries, dates, and even dried pears—also complement the taste of almond and can be used if you prefer.

Be sure to use pure almond paste rather than almond filling. Almond paste is usually sold in 7-ounce tubes or 8-ounce cans; either amount works just fine in this recipe.

1¼ cups dried red cherries
3½ cups cake flour
1½ teaspoons baking powder
1 teaspoon baking soda
¼ teaspoon salt
7 to 8 ounces pure almond paste
1¼ cups granulated sugar
2 sticks unsalted butter, softened
5 large eggs
1 cup sour cream
1 tablespoon Amaretto or pure vanilla
   extract
Confectioners' sugar

Heat the oven to 325°F. Butter a 12-cup bundt pan and dust the inside with flour. Put the dried cherries in a small dish, cover them with hot water, and let them stand 20 to 30 minutes until they are soft and plump. Drain well, pat dry, and then chop them fine.

Sift the flour, baking powder, baking soda, and salt together and set aside.

Combine the almond paste and granulated sugar with an electric mixer until the almond paste is completely granular and well blended with the sugar. Add the butter and mix on high speed until the mixture is light and fluffy, 2 to 3 minutes. Add the eggs, one at a time, mixing well after each addition. Add the sour cream and Amaretto or vanilla and mix to combine. Stop the mixer and add the dry ingredients. Mix just until blended and then fold in the chopped cherries.

Transfer the batter to the prepared pan and smooth the top with a rubber spatula. Bake until a toothpick inserted in the center comes out clean, 55 to 60 minutes. Cool the cake in the pan 5 minutes and then invert it onto a wire rack and remove the pan. When the cake is completely cool, sift confectioners' sugar over the top.

Annie Apple Cake

Makes 1 10-inch bundt cake
10 to 12 servings

No time of year seems more perfect to make an apple cake than autumn, when fresh, tart apples and apple cider are abundant. This cake is moist and dense, filled with fruit and nuts and doubly flavored with the snap of tart apple. The glaze is thick, rich, and irresistible.

CAKE
2 cups light brown sugar
2 sticks unsalted butter, softened
2 large eggs
2 cups apple cider, at room
*   temperature*
2 teaspoons pure vanilla extract
3 cups unbleached all-purpose flour
2½ teaspoons baking soda
1½ teaspoons cinnamon
¼ teaspoon salt
¼ teaspoon ground allspice
¾ cup chopped dates
¾ cup chopped unpeeled apple
¾ cup chopped toasted pecans or
*   walnuts*
¾ cup raisins

GLAZE
½ cup light brown sugar
5 tablespoons unsalted butter
¼ cup apple cider
¼ cup sour cream

Place a rack in the center of the oven and preheat the oven to 350°F. Generously butter a 12-cup bundt pan. (This cake has a tendency to stick to the pan if you don't use enough butter, so don't skimp.) Dust the inside of the pan with flour and tap out the excess.

Using an electric mixer on high speed, cream the brown sugar and butter until light and fluffy, 2 to 3 minutes. Add the eggs, one at a time, mixing well after each addition. Turn the mixer to low speed and add the cider and vanilla. Mix well. In another bowl, stir the flour, baking soda, cinnamon, salt, and allspice together. Add it to the creamed mixture and mix lightly. Add the dates, apple, nuts, and raisins and fold together.

Transfer the batter to the prepared pan. Bake until a toothpick inserted in the center comes out clean, 55 to 60 minutes. Cool the cake in the pan 10 minutes and then turn it out onto a wire rack. Let it cool completely before glazing it.

To make the glaze, combine all the ingredients in a small pan. Heat to a boil and then cook vigorously for 4 minutes. Remove the pan from the heat and let it stand 5 minutes. Place the rack with the cake on it over a sheet of waxed paper. Spoon the glaze over the top of the cake, letting it drip over the sides.

Banana Cake Roll

Makes 1 cake roll
10 servings

Most banana cakes are layered affairs, swathed in a rich cloak of frosting. This one is a delicate and airy sponge roll, filled with a cloud of rum-flavored whipped cream. It can be garnished with fresh fruit or simply embellished with a shower of confectioners' sugar. Either way, it is a sensational cake.

CAKE
1 large very ripe banana
2 tablespoons sour cream
1 teaspoon pure vanilla extract
¾ cup plus 2 tablespoons cake flour
½ teaspoon baking soda
⅛ teaspoon baking powder
Pinch salt
⅔ stick (5⅓ tablespoons) unsalted
  butter, softened
½ cup granulated sugar
1 large egg

FILLING
1 cup whipping cream
2 tablespoons sour cream
3 tablespoons confectioners' sugar
2 teaspoons dark rum
1 teaspoon pure vanilla extract
½ cup finely diced ripe banana

Heat the oven to 375°F. Line a 12″ × 15″ pan (this is slightly smaller than a standard-sized jelly roll pan) with a length of aluminum foil that extends three inches beyond both short ends of the pan. Grease the foil and coat it with a fine dusting of flour.

Mash the banana with a fork until it is almost, but not quite, smooth. There should be some lumps in it. Measure out ⅔ cup to use in this recipe and put it in a medium-sized bowl. Add the sour cream and vanilla and mix well. Set aside.

In a separate bowl, sift the flour, baking soda, baking powder, and salt together and set aside.

Cream the butter and granulated sugar with an electric mixer on high speed until smooth, 1 to 2 minutes. Add the egg and mix well. Add the banana mixture and mix lightly to combine. Finally, add the flour mixture and gently fold it in.

Transfer the batter to the prepared pan, using a rubber spatula to spread it into a smooth, even layer. Bake just until the cake is set in the center, 9 to 11 minutes. Remove the cake from the oven and cover it with a sheet of aluminum foil. Lift the cake from the pan by using the overhang of the foil. Transfer the foil-covered cake to a cooling rack and let it cool completely. For the best results, the cake should be filled and rolled as soon as it reaches room temperature.

While the cake is cooling, prepare the filling. Whip the cream and sour cream until the mixture holds soft peaks. Add the sugar, rum, and vanilla. Continue beating until it is stiff enough to hold its shape. Gently fold in the diced banana.

Remove the top piece of foil and spread the filling evenly over the cake. Starting at a long side, roll the cake up as a jelly roll, using the bottom sheet of foil to help you. As you are rolling the cake, separate the foil from the cake. Carefully transfer the rolled cake, seam side down, to a serving plate. Cover the cake with a large sheet of plastic wrap and work through the wrap to compact the cake and neaten the roll. Sift a generous coating of confectioners' sugar over the top. To serve, cut the cake on a slight diagonal, using a serrated knife.

Lemon Velvet Cake

Makes 1 8-inch bundt cake
8 servings

Lemon cakes are timeless in their appeal. Their clean, fresh flavor and zesty tang provide a good foil for the richness that comes from butter and eggs. This cake is moist and light and has an exceptionally fine, tight crumb. The fresh lemon flavor shines through both in the cake and in its thin glaze.

CAKE
2 cups cake flour
1 cup granulated sugar
¼ teaspoon baking soda
1 teaspoon baking powder
¼ teaspoon salt
2 sticks unsalted butter, softened
4 large eggs
5 tablespoons fresh lemon juice
Finely grated zest of 2 lemons

GLAZE
1 cup confectioners' sugar
2 to 3 tablespoons fresh lemon juice

Heat the oven to 350°F. Generously butter an 8-inch tube or bundt pan. (Note that an 8-inch pan is smaller than most standard pans of these types.)

Combine the flour, granulated sugar, baking soda, baking powder, and salt in the bowl of an electric mixer. Mix on low speed for 20 seconds or until the ingredients are combined. Cut the butter into tablespoon-size pieces and add them to the dry ingredients. Mix on low speed until the butter is mixed in, about 20 seconds. The batter will not look smooth. Add the eggs, lemon juice, and lemon zest. Mix on high speed for 3 minutes.

Transfer the batter to the prepared pan. Bake until a toothpick inserted in the center comes out clean, 35 to 40 minutes. Let the cake cool in the pan for 10 minutes, and then invert the cake onto a wire rack and remove the pan. Cool the cake completely before adding the glaze.

To make the glaze, sift the confectioners' sugar into a small bowl. Add 2 tablespoons lemon juice and mix until smooth. The glaze should be slightly thinner than whipping cream. If it is thicker, add additional lemon juice. Spoon the glaze over the top of the cake, letting it drip down the sides.

Peaches and Cream Cake

Makes 1 9-inch layer cake
10 servings

This is an old-fashioned prize winner, a towering two-layer cake that adds an extra-special touch to summertime celebrations. Two golden rich layers are painted with a peachy syrup for additional moisture and flavor. Sliced peaches and a cloud of whipped cream finish it nicely.

CAKE
1 cup buttermilk
1 teaspoon baking soda
2 cups cake flour
2¼ teaspoons baking powder
½ teaspoon salt
1⅓ cups granulated sugar
1½ sticks unsalted butter, softened
3 large eggs, separated
2 teaspoons grated lemon zest
¼ teaspoon cream of tartar

FILLING
2 to 3 large ripe peaches, about
  1 pound total
¼ to ⅓ cup granulated sugar
Juice of 1 lemon
¼ cup peach schnapps

TOPPING
1½ cups whipping cream
¼ cup confectioners' sugar
¼ cup peach schnapps

Heat the oven to 350°F. Butter two 9-inch round layer cake pans, line the bottoms with a circle of waxed paper, and butter the paper. Stir the buttermilk and baking soda together and set aside while you start the cake. Sift the flour, baking powder, and salt together and set aside.

Cream the granulated sugar and butter with an electric mixer on high speed until the mixture is light and fluffy. Add the egg yolks and mix 2 minutes longer. Stop the mixer and add the buttermilk mixture and lemon zest. Mix on low speed just enough to combine. Add the sifted dry ingredients.

With a clean mixer, beat the egg whites on low speed until they are foamy. Add the cream of tartar and increase the speed to high. Beat until the whites hold soft peaks; then gently but thoroughly fold them into the batter.

Divide the batter between the prepared pans and smooth the tops with a rubber spatula. Bake until a toothpick inserted in the center comes out clean, 22 to 25 minutes.

While the cakes are baking, peel and pit the peaches and cut them into ⅜-inch slices. Place the slices in a medium-sized bowl and mix in the granulated sugar, lemon juice, and schnapps.

When the cakes have finished baking, remove them from the oven. Cool them in the pans for 5 minutes and then invert the cakes onto a rack; remove the pan and waxed paper. While the cakes are still warm, brush them with some of the liquid from the peaches, applying a generous coat every few minutes. Set aside to cool completely. Cover and refrigerate the peaches.

To make the topping, whip the cream until it holds soft peaks. Add the confectioners' sugar and schnapps and mix a bit longer, until the cream stiffens to a spreadable consistency but is not yet buttery.

To assemble the cake, carefully transfer one layer to a cake plate and spread about ½ cup of the whipped cream over it. Arrange the peaches over the cream. Top with the second layer. Spread the remaining whipped cream over the top and sides of the cake. Refrigerate 1 hour before serving so the cake sets up. If it is refrigerated longer, let it stand at room temperature for 15 to 20 minutes before it is served.

Spicy Lemon Gingerbread

Makes 1 ring cake
6 to 8 servings

This is the best gingerbread I know—light, sprightly, and fresh. Unlike many other cakes of this type, it has a very soft texture and a lively flavor. It's quite easy to make, although one caution is in order: the cake really wants to stick to the pan. The only way to avoid its sticking is to make doubly sure you use enough grease on the pan.

1 piece fresh ginger, about 1¼ inches
  square
½ cup granulated sugar
Finely grated zest of 1 very large or 2
  small lemons
1 large egg
1 stick unsalted butter, softened
½ cup sour cream
½ cup dark corn syrup
1 cup unbleached all-purpose flour
1¼ teaspoons baking soda
¼ teaspoon cinnamon
¼ teaspoon ground allspice
¼ teaspoon salt
Whipped cream or Creamy Custard
  Sauce (see Index)

Heat the oven to 350°F. Generously grease a 6- to 7-cup ring mold and dust the inside with flour.

Peel the ginger with a vegetable peeler. Cut it into chunks and mince it as finely as possible in a food processor. Add the sugar and lemon zest and process until the ginger and zest are very finely minced. Add the egg and butter and process 1 minute. Stop the processor and add the sour cream and corn syrup. Process 10 seconds. Remove the cover and add the flour, baking soda, cinnamon, allspice, and salt; process just until they are blended together.

If you prefer to use an electric mixer instead of a food processor, proceed this way: Mince the ginger and lemon zest as fine as possible and set aside. Cream the butter and sugar until light with the mixer on high speed, 2 minutes. Add the egg and mix 1 minute longer. Turn to low speed and mix in the sour cream and corn syrup. Stop the mixer. Add the flour, baking soda, cinnamon, allspice, salt, ginger, and lemon zest. Mix just until combined.

Transfer the batter to the prepared pan. Bake until a toothpick inserted in the center comes out clean, about 30 minutes. Serve with a dollop of whipped cream or lemon-flavored custard sauce.

Strawberry Shortcake

Makes 8 servings

This grand creation of flaky biscuit, tart/sweet berries, and clouds of whipped cream is as down-home good as dessert will ever be. As proper at a Fourth of July fireworks celebration as it is at the fanciest dinner party, it is, in short, nearly perfect.

Doubtless there will be eyebrows raised when some people see balsamic vinegar as an ingredient, but Italians have added this intensely flavored vinegar to berries for centuries and the results are remarkable. A mere whiff of it elevates the scent and flavor of strawberries to what they were surely intended to be. Certainly it can be left out.

BERRIES
2 pints strawberries
Granulated sugar to taste
Drop or two of balsamic vinegar, if
desired

SUGAR BISCUITS
2 cups unbleached all-purpose flour
3½ tablespoons granulated sugar
1 tablespoon baking powder
¼ teaspoon salt
1 stick unsalted butter, chilled
¾ cup plus 2 tablespoons half-and-half

FILLING AND TOPPING
1½ cups whipping cream
2 tablespoons confectioners' sugar

At least an hour before they are to be served, wash the berries and then hull them. Place eight or ten soft berries in a medium-sized bowl with a bit of sugar and mash them with a fork. Slice the rest of the berries into the bowl, add sugar to taste (start with about 2 tablespoons per pint of berries and use more, if desired), and add a bit of balsamic vinegar, if you wish. Let the berries stand so they become juicy—they can be prepared several hours in advance.

Place the rack in the center of the oven and preheat the oven to 425°F. Have an ungreased baking sheet ready.

For the biscuits, sift the flour, 3 tablespoons granulated sugar, baking powder, and salt into a large bowl. Cut the butter into small pieces and add it to the flour mixture. Blend the pieces in with a pastry blender until the mixture is coarse and mealy. Add ¾ cup of the half-and-half and stir just until the dough begins to mass together.

The biscuits can be made in a food processor. Combine the dry ingredients in the work bowl. Add the butter, cut in small pieces, and process until the butter is the size of small peas. Remove the cover and add ¾ cup of the half-and-half. Process briefly, just until the dough clumps together.

With lightly floured hands, gather the dough into a ball. Transfer it to a lightly floured board and roll it into a circle about 1½ inches thick. Cut into 3-inch biscuits. Reroll and cut the scraps. Transfer the biscuits to an ungreased baking sheet, brush them lightly with the remaining half-and-half, and sprinkle the remaining granulated sugar on the tops.

Bake until the biscuits are golden, 12 to 15 minutes. Transfer them to a wire rack and cool slightly.

To serve, whip the cream until it holds soft peaks and mix in the confectioners' sugar. Split the biscuits—shortcakes—in half. Divide the berries among them and top with a dollop of whipped cream. Replace the covers and spoon a generous mound of whipped cream over the tops. Serve immediately.

Forty-Karat Carrot Cake

Makes 1 10-inch cake
10 to 12 servings

There are many renditions of carrot cake and, quite frankly, it's hard to find a bad one. This one, though, is the cream of the crop. It is moist, spicy, and tender, baked in a bundt pan so it is big and impressive.

For many, the cream cheese icing is the raison d'etre of carrot cakes. This time it shows up as a creamy, smooth glaze that glosses over the cake. The cake also can be baked in three 8-inch layer cake pans and frosted with a traditional cream cheese frosting, if you prefer.

CAKE
4 to 5 medium carrots
1 tablespoon fresh lemon juice
1 medium seedless orange
1⅔ cups granulated sugar
1¼ cups vegetable oil
4 large eggs
1 tablespoon cinnamon
2¼ teaspoons baking soda
½ teaspoon salt
¼ teaspoon grated nutmeg
¼ teaspoon ground allspice
1 cup chopped toasted pecans or
  walnuts
¾ cup raisins
2 cups unbleached all-purpose flour

CREAM CHEESE GLAZE
3 ounces cream cheese
1 cup confectioners' sugar
1 teaspoon pure vanilla extract
4 tablespoons orange juice

Heat the oven to 325°F. Generously butter a 12-cup bundt pan.

Grate the carrots in a food processor or with the largest holes of a four-sided grater. Measure out 3 packed cups to use in this recipe and toss them with the lemon juice. Cut a flat top and bottom on the orange and stand it on a cutting board. Using a small sharp knife, cut away all the rind and white pith. Coarsely chop the orange and add it along with any juice to the carrots.

In a large food processor or with an electric mixer, mix the granulated sugar, oil, and eggs for 2 to 3 minutes. Add the cinnamon, baking soda, salt, nutmeg, and allspice, and mix well. Stop the processor or mixer and add the carrots, orange, nuts, and raisins. Mix just enough to combine. Add the flour and mix in lightly.

Transfer the batter to the prepared pan. Bake until a toothpick inserted in the center comes out clean, 55 to 60 minutes. Cool the cake in the pan for 10 minutes and then invert the cake onto a wire rack. Remove the pan and cool the cake completely before glazing it.

To make the glaze, mix the cream cheese and confectioners' sugar with an electric mixer until smooth. Add the vanilla and 4 tablespoons orange juice and mix until completely smooth. The glaze should be of a consistency that will coat the cake and also drip gently over the sides. Adjust the amount of juice until that point is reached. Spoon the glaze over the cake, letting it drip down the sides.

Flavors of Christmas Cake

Makes 1 8-inch cake
6 to 8 servings

All holidays have their own traditions, many of them centered on the celebratory foods of the season. This luscious eggnog-flavored cake, swirled with a ribbon of cranberry relish, is a delicious one to add to your holiday menus. It makes a festive dessert or brunch-time coffeecake, and is perfect for serving any time throughout the Christmas season.

For an eye-catching garnish, add some colored sugar or a tinted glaze to the top of the cake. Then cover the edge of the serving plate with seasonal greenery and cranberries.

CRANBERRY RELISH
¾ cup cranberries
⅓ cup granulated sugar
⅓ cup pecans
2 tablespoons flour
1 tablespoon brandy

CAKE
2 large eggs
1 cup granulated sugar
1 stick unsalted butter, softened
⅓ cup commercial eggnog or whipping
   cream
2 tablespoons brandy
1 teaspoon pure vanilla extract
1¼ cups unbleached all-purpose flour
½ teaspoon freshly grated nutmeg
½ teaspoon baking soda
¼ teaspoon salt
¼ teaspoon cinnamon
¼ teaspoon mace
Confectioners' sugar

Heat the oven to 350°F. Butter an 8-inch springform pan.

Prepare the relish by combining the cranberries, granulated sugar, pecans, flour, and brandy in a food processor with the metal blade. Process until the berries are finely chopped. Remove the mixture from the processor and set aside. Wipe out the work bowl with a paper towel.

To make the cake, add the eggs and granulated sugar to the processor and mix for 1 minute. Add the butter and mix another minute. Add the eggnog or whipping cream, brandy, and vanilla and mix 10 seconds. Remove the cover and add the flour, nutmeg, baking soda, salt, cinnamon, and mace. Mix in by turning the processor on and off in short spurts, just until combined.

Spoon about ⅔ of the batter into the prepared pan and spread it in an even layer. Spoon the relish over the top, and swirl it in with the point of a sharp knife. Top with the remaining batter and spread it carefully.

Bake until a toothpick inserted in the center of the cake (not the relish) comes out clean, 50 to 55 minutes. Cool completely and then remove the sides from the pan. Sift confectioners' sugar over the top at serving time.

Boston Cream Pie

Makes 1 8-inch cake
8 servings

One could argue about whether Boston cream pie is a cake or a pie, but there is no disputing its enduring popularity. It has been passionately adored since the very first time it was served at the Parker House Hotel in Boston.

Over the years, I've made subtle changes to the classic version and have found that a hint of orange in the cake and filling is a perfect addition.

CAKE
1½ cups cake flour
¾ teaspoon baking powder
1 stick unsalted butter, softened
1 cup granulated sugar
2 teaspoons pure vanilla extract
2 large eggs
Finely grated zest of ½ orange
½ cup whipping cream

FILLING
1 large egg
2½ tablespoons all-purpose flour
6 tablespoons granulated sugar
¾ cup milk
¼ cup orange juice
1 tablespoon unsalted butter
2 teaspoons pure vanilla extract
¼ cup mini chocolate chips, if desired

GLAZE
4 ounces semisweet chocolate
¼ cup confectioners' sugar
2 tablespoons sour cream

Preheat the oven to 350°F. Butter an 8-inch springform pan.

Sift the flour and baking powder together and set aside. Beat the butter, granulated sugar, and vanilla with an electric mixer on high speed until light, about 2 minutes. Add the eggs, one at a time, mixing well after each addition, and then mix in the orange zest and cream. Stop the mixer and add the sifted dry ingredients. Gently fold them in with a rubber spatula.

Transfer the batter to the prepared pan. Bake until a toothpick inserted in the center comes out clean, 38 to 42 minutes. Place the pan on a wire rack and cool to room temperature.

To prepare the filling, whisk the egg in a heavy saucepan. Add the flour and granulated sugar and mix well. Turn the heat to medium low and begin cooking, whisking constantly. Cook until the mixture is warmed, and then whisk in the milk. Continue cooking, stirring with a wooden spoon, until the mixture is quite thick. Remove from the heat, add the orange juice, butter, and vanilla. Stir until the butter is melted. Cool to room temperature and then fold in the chocolate chips, if you are including them. Place a piece of plastic wrap directly on the surface and refrigerate until well chilled or up to 2 days.

Shortly before assembling the cake, melt the chocolate for the glaze. Press the confectioners' sugar through a fine strainer into the chocolate. Add the sour cream and mix well.

To assemble, remove the sides from the springform pan. Level the cake if it is mounded in the center. Then, using a long serrated knife, split the layer in half horizontally. Spread the chilled custard filling over the bottom half and carefully replace the top layer. Spread the chocolate glaze over the top. The cake should stand for at least an hour before it is served. For longer storage, cover the cake and refrigerate it. Let it come to room temperature before you serve it.

Creamy Cheesecake

Makes 1 10-inch cake
10 to 12 servings

Discover perfection in a cheesecake. Its texture is sublime—smooth, creamy, and dense—the flavor rich and straightforward. It bakes quickly, never cracks, serves a crowd, and freezes well.

There are various ways to personalize the recipe, starting with the crust. Here it's made with butter cookies, but amaretti biscuits are a great choice, in which case you'd probably be tempted to add a splash of amaretto to the filling. Oreo cookies or chocolate wafers add a subtle suggestion of chocolate. That theme can be carried further by folding some mini chocolate chips into the filling. In the summer, I like to use lemon cookies for the crust and—you guessed it—I add some lemon zest and lemon juice to the filling.

A food processor is a godsend when it comes to making the creamiest cheesecakes. Use it if you have one. Otherwise use an electric mixer, making sure to beat the mixture for a full 5 minutes.

Fresh fruit is a natural accompaniment, either added as a jewel-like topping or as a sauce. Of course, it's just fine plain. In any event, the cake is a winner.

CRUST
4 ounces good quality butter cookies
(I use Pepperidge Farm Chessman
  cookies)
3 tablespoons unsalted butter, melted

FILLING
3 large eggs
1¼ cups granulated sugar
2½ pounds (five 8-ounce packages)
  cream cheese, softened
1 tablespoon pure vanilla extract

Heat the oven to 350°F. Have a 10-inch springform pan ready. To be on the safe side, wrap aluminum foil around the bottom of the pan in case the filling seeps out a bit.

For the crust, crush the cookies in a food processor until they are powdery. Add the butter and mix well. Transfer the crumbs to the pan and press them evenly into the bottom only. Set aside. Wipe out the processor work bowl with a paper towel so there aren't any crumbs left in it.

For the filling, mix the eggs and sugar in a food processor or with an electric mixer for 1 minute. Add the cream cheese and vanilla, in batches if necessary, depending on the size of your processor. Mix 2 full minutes in the processor or 5 minutes with the mixer, stopping several times, no matter which one you use, to clean down the sides of the bowl with a rubber spatula.

Transfer the batter to the prepared pan and smooth the top with a rubber spatula. Bake until the cake is slightly puffy at the edges but is still slightly soft and creamy in the center, 33 to 35 minutes. Transfer the pan to a wire rack and cool to room temperature. Cover and refrigerate at least 6 hours before serving.

Peter, Peter Pumpkin Cheesecake

Makes 1 10-inch cake
10 to 12 servings

This is a classic, a creamy cheesecake that stands ready to challenge pumpkin pie as the favorite Thanksgiving dessert. You don't have to dig too deeply to figure out why it has become so popular. The luxurious texture of cheesecake takes on the perennially favorite flavor of pumpkin with superb results.

Canned pumpkin works very well in this recipe, so don't feel guilty that you're not cooking and pureeing a sugar pumpkin.

CRUST
2 ounces cookies (I use Pepperidge
  Farm Bordeaux cookies)
2 tablespoons unsalted butter, melted

FILLING
3 large eggs
1 cup granulated sugar
1½ pounds (three 8-ounce packages)
  cream cheese, softened
1½ cups solid-pack canned pumpkin
1 tablespoon cornstarch
1 tablespoon pure vanilla extract
1 tablespoon bourbon or Cointreau
½ teaspoon cinnamon
⅛ teaspoon ground allspice
Freshly grated nutmeg

TOPPING
2 cups sour cream
¼ cup granulated sugar
2 teaspoons bourbon or Cointreau

Heat the oven to 350°F. Have a 10-inch springform pan ready.

For the crust, finely crush the cookies in a food processor or blender. Mix the crumbs with the melted butter. Transfer them to the springform pan and press into an even layer over the bottom of the pan. Set aside.

For the filling, mix the eggs and sugar in a food processor or with an electric mixer for 1 minute. Add the cream cheese (in batches in the processor, if necessary) and mix at least 2 minutes in the processor, 5 minutes with the mixer. Add the pumpkin, cornstarch, vanilla, bourbon or Cointreau, cinnamon, allspice, and nutmeg and mix well.

Transfer the mixture to the pan. Wrap the bottom of the pan in aluminum foil so there's no chance the filling will leak out. Bake until the cake is set at the edges but still somewhat soft in the center, about 50 minutes.

While the cake is baking, prepare the topping. Mix the sour cream with the sugar and flavoring until smooth. After the cake has baked, remove it from the oven and let it cool 5 minutes. Gently spread the topping evenly over the top. Return the cake to the oven and bake 5 to 7 minutes longer. Cool the cheesecake on a wire rack and then cover it tightly and refrigerate 4 hours or overnight before serving.

Dailey's Irish Cream Cheesecake

Makes 1 10-inch cake
12 servings

Many ingredients are called upon to flavor cheesecakes. Over the last several years, one of the most popular additions has been Irish cream liqueur. Its mild yet seductive taste melds perfectly into the rich, creamy cheese base of this dessert.

CRUST
5½ ounces chocolate cookies (I use
Pepperidge Farm Brownie Chocolate
Nut)
4 tablespoons unsalted butter, melted

FILLING
1 cup plus 2 tablespoons granulated
sugar
3 large eggs
2 pounds (four 8-ounce packages)
cream cheese, softened
¾ cup Irish cream liqueur
1 tablespoon unsweetened cocoa powder
1 tablespoon cornstarch
1 teaspoon instant espresso coffee
dissolved in ½ teaspoon hot water
1 teaspoon pure vanilla extract

TOPPING
2 cups sour cream
¼ cup granulated sugar
3 tablespoons Irish cream liqueur

Heat the oven to 350°F. Have a 10-inch springform pan ready.

Crush the cookies into fine crumbs in a food processor or blender. Add the butter and mix well. Transfer the crumbs to the pan and press them into an even layer over the bottom of the pan. Bake until the crumbs are set, about 10 minutes. Set aside to cool.

For the filling, mix the sugar and eggs in a food processor or with an electric mixer for 1 to 2 minutes. Add the cream cheese (in batches in the processor, if necessary) and mix until thoroughly smooth, 2 to 3 minutes in a processor, longer with a mixer. Add the liqueur, cocoa, cornstarch, coffee mixture, and vanilla and mix well.

Pour the filling into the crust. Bake until the cake is just set in the center, about 35 to 40 minutes. Remove the cake from the oven and cool for 5 minutes, but do not turn off the oven.

For the topping, combine the sour cream, sugar, and liqueur and mix well, making sure to smooth out all the lumps in the sour cream.

When the cheesecake has cooled for 5 minutes, gently pour the topping over the cake and spread it out in an even layer. Bake 6 minutes. Cool to room temperature and then cover and refrigerate the cheesecake for at least 4 hours before serving.

5
Pies and Tarts

Basic Single-Crust Pastry

Old-Fashioned Butter Flake Pastry

Chocolate Turkle Pie

Chocolate Almond Brickle Pie

Sweet P'tater Pie

Autumn Apple Cranberry Pie

Key Lime Pie

Citrus Tart

Summer Jewels Fruit Tart

Caramel Pecan Tart

Basic Single-Crust Pastry

Makes 1 single-crust pie shell, 9 inches in diameter
or
1 single-crust tart shell, up to 10 inches in diameter

This is a foolproof pastry recipe that has a buttery taste and flaky texture. Use it for delicate pies and tarts, both sweet and savory.

> *1 stick unsalted butter, chilled*
> *1 large egg yolk*
> *1 tablespoon granulated sugar (see*
> * Note)*
> *¼ teaspoon salt*
> *5 tablespoons ice water*
> *1½ cups unbleached all-purpose flour*

To make the pastry in a food processor, cut the butter into tablespoon-size pieces. Place the butter in the work bowl and process several seconds to chop coarsely. Add the egg yolk, sugar, salt, and water. Process several seconds, just until the ingredients are combined and the butter is chopped to the size of small peas. Add the flour and process until the dough clumps together.

To make by hand, combine the flour, sugar, and salt in a medium-sized bowl. Cut the butter into small bits and add it to the flour. Cut the butter in with a pastry blender until it is chopped to the size of small peas. Mix the egg yolk and water in a small dish and pour it over the flour mixture. Mix with a fork just until the dough clumps together.

Transfer the dough to a large plastic food bag. Working through the bag, shape the dough into a ball and then flatten it into a disk. Refrigerate it until it is firm enough to roll.

On a floured board roll the dough out in a circle to fit the pie or tart pan of your choice. Ease the dough into the pan and press it gently into the edges. Trim the excess dough, leaving it about ¼ inch beyond the top rim of the pie plate or tart pan. Pinch the edge, if desired, to make a decorative edge. Place the crust in the refrigerator for 15 minutes before baking.

To prebake the pastry, heat the oven to 400°F. Prick the pastry at random with the tines of a fork (the holes will later let steam escape). Line the pastry with a single sheet of aluminum foil and fill the foil with dried beans. Place the pan on a baking sheet and bake the crust in the preheated oven for 12 minutes. Remove the foil with the dried beans. Return the crust to the oven and bake until it is lightly browned, 10 to 12 minutes longer.

Note: For savory recipes, omit the sugar.

Old-Fashioned Butter Flake Pastry

Makes 1 9-inch double-crust pie shell

This is an old-fashioned pie crust, flaky, light, and tender. It is best used with fruit pies.

¼ cup unsalted butter, well chilled
½ cup solid vegetable shortening
1 teaspoon granulated sugar
½ teaspoon salt
1 large egg yolk
⅓ cup ice water
2¼ cups unbleached all-purpose flour

To use a food processor, combine the butter (cut in pieces), the shortening, sugar, salt, egg yolk, and water in the work bowl. Process several seconds, until the butter and shortening are chopped and all the ingredients mixed. Add the flour and process just until the dough clumps together.

To make the pastry by hand, combine the flour, sugar, and salt in a large mixing bowl. Cut the butter into small pieces and add it to the bowl along with the shortening. Using a pastry blender, work the shortening and butter into the flour until the mixture is coarse and granular. Combine the egg yolk and water. Add them to the bowl, mixing just until the dough masses together into a ball.

Gather the dough and divide it into two parts, one slightly larger than the other. Transfer each part to separate large plastic food bags. Working through the bag, shape the dough into a ball and then flatten it into a disk. Refrigerate both disks until well chilled so they will be easier to roll.

On a floured board, roll the larger piece of dough into a circle to fit a 9-inch pie plate. The exact size of the circle will be determined by the depth of the pie plate. Roll it so it is large enough to drape over the sides. Transfer it to the pie plate, leaving the overhang intact. When placing the dough in the pan, ease it into the bottom and up the sides. Do not stretch or pull the dough or it is likely to shrink back when it bakes.

Fill the crust as desired and then roll out the top piece of dough into a circle slightly larger than the diameter of the pie plate. Gently place it over the filling and press it to seal the crust. Trim the excess and crimp an attractive edge. Bake as directed in the pie recipe you are using.

Chocolate Turkle Pie

Makes 1 9-inch pie
8 servings

This is the type of dessert we dream of. What more could anyone ask? Soft, rich, oozingly wonderful caramel, lots of creamy, smooth chocolate, and morsels of flavorful, crunchy pecans. The recipe's name is a paean to turtle candies that just for fun we used to call turkles.

CRUST
2 cups toasted pecans
¼ cup granulated sugar
4 tablespoons unsalted butter, melted

FILLING
1 pound caramel candy (see Note)
¼ cup whipping cream
1 cup coarsely chopped toasted pecans

TOPPING
8 ounces semisweet chocolate
⅓ cup whipping cream
¼ cup confectioners' sugar

Heat the oven to 350°F. Have a 9-inch pie plate ready.

For the crust, mince the pecans with the granulated sugar in a food processor until they are finely minced but not ground. Mix in the butter. Remove the mixture and press it evenly into the bottom and up the sides of the pie plate. Bake the crust until it is lightly browned, 12 to 15 minutes. Cool it completely before filling.

For the filling, melt the caramel with the cream in a double boiler, stirring until smooth, or in a microwave oven, stirring often. Cool to lukewarm and then pour the caramel into the crust. Sprinkle pecans evenly over the top.

For the topping, melt the chocolate with the cream and sugar in the top of a double boiler, stirring until smooth, or in a microwave oven, stirring often. Pour the topping over the pie, smoothing the surface with a rubber spatula. Refrigerate the pie at least 4 hours or up to 2 days before serving it.

Note: If at all possible, try to use bulk caramel (I use Nestlé's Caramel, which can be purchased at some specialty food stores. I order mine from Maid of Scandinavia, in Minnesota, 612/927-7996.) Its flavor and texture are far superior to those of individually wrapped caramel candies.

Chocolate Almond Brickle Pie

Makes 1 8-inch pie
8 servings

What could be better than a big chocolate candy bar baked as a pie? This old-fashioned favorite is filled to capacity with bits of toffee, chocolate chips, and nuts. Kids adore it, and adults are hardly immune to its charms, either. It will keep beautifully in the freezer for several months—if it's given the chance. But be cautioned: It's just the type of thing everybody likes to nibble when the urge for something sweet hits.

*5 ounces sweet baking chocolate (I use
  Ghirardelli dark sweet)*
½ cup granulated sugar
¼ cup water
3 large eggs
1½ sticks unsalted butter, softened
1 tablespoon pure vanilla extract
*1 package (6 ounces) almond brickle
  chips (I use Heath Bits)*
½ cup chopped toasted pecans
½ cup chocolate chips
*3 tablespoons unbleached all-purpose
  flour*

Heat the oven to 350°F. Butter an 8-inch pie plate. Melt the chocolate with the sugar and water in the top of a double boiler or in a microwave oven.

Transfer the chocolate to a large bowl and cool slightly. Beat the eggs, add them to the chocolate, and mix with an electric mixer on medium speed until well-blended. Add the butter and vanilla and mix 1 minute or until smooth and fluffy.

Stop the mixer and add the brickle chips, pecans, chocolate chips, and flour. Fold them in with a large rubber spatula.

Transfer the mixture to the prepared pan and smooth the top with a rubber spatula. Bake until the pie is set around the edges but is still somewhat soft in the center, 22 to 27 minutes. Cool it completely and then cover tightly and refrigerate at least 4 hours before serving. To serve, cut into wedges.

Sweet P'tater Pie

Makes 1 9-inch pie
8 servings

It took me a long time to appreciate sweet potatoes, but once I realized that you didn't have to drown them in sugar and tiny marshmallows, I thought they were just fine as a vegetable. Later, when I learned they could be served as a dessert, well, whole new avenues opened up.

This is one of those avenues, a fine route to take in the fall when sweet potatoes are abundant. A fluffy mound of mashed sweet potatoes is mixed with sugar, spice, and other things nice and baked into a most delightful pie. It is at its very best when it's served with a dollop of whipped cream that has been gently sweetened and laced with a touch of bourbon.

> *1 prebaked Basic Single-Crust Pastry*
>   *pie shell (see Index)*
> *2 cups mashed sweet potatoes (see Note)*
> *½ cup granulated sugar*
> *3 large eggs*
> *3 tablespoons unsalted butter, melted*
> *3 tablespoons maple syrup*
> *3 tablespoons bourbon*
> *1½ teaspoons pumpkin pie spice*
> *¼ teaspoon salt*
> *1¼ cups half-and-half*
> *Whipped cream, flavored with*
>   *bourbon, for serving, if desired*

Heat the oven to 375°F.

Combine the mashed sweet potatoes, sugar, eggs, butter, syrup, bourbon, spice, and salt in a food processor and process until the mixture is completely smooth.

Add ½ cup of the half-and-half (if you have a large processor, add all of the half-and-half) and mix well. Transfer mixture to a large mixing bowl and add the remaining half-and-half. Whisk until smooth.

Pour the filling into the prebaked pastry. Bake until the filling is just set in the center, 50 to 55 minutes. Cool the pie to room temperature and then refrigerate at least 4 hours before serving. Serve with a dollop of whipped cream flavored with bourbon.

Note: About 2 pounds of sweet potatoes will make 2 cups of cooked mashed potatoes. They can either be cooked in the microwave oven or baked until they are soft. When they are cool enough to handle, scoop out and measure the flesh.

Autumn Apple Cranberry Pie

Makes 1 9-inch pie
6 to 8 servings

This is a doozy of an apple pie. The crust is flaky and light, the filling tart, sweet, spicy, and just right. The cranberry sauce lends a rosy glow and gives an agreeable tang to the apples.

For the best-tasting pie, I like to use several different types of apples. Try one MacIntosh with a few Jonathans, and a Granny Smith thrown in for good measure.

CRUST
1 batch Old-Fashioned Butter Flake
Pastry (see Index)

FILLING
1 to 1¼ cups granulated sugar
1½ tablespoons unbleached all-purpose
flour
1½ tablespoons cornstarch
1 teaspoon cinnamon
¼ teaspoon freshly grated nutmeg
¼ teaspoon ground allspice
Pinch salt
2 pounds tart baking apples
1 cup whole berry cranberry relish,
preferably homemade (see Index)
⅓ cup dried currants
2 tablespoons unsalted butter

GLAZE
1½ tablespoons whipping cream
1 tablespoon granulated sugar
Dash cinnamon

Heat the oven to 400°F. Have a 9-inch pie plate at hand.

Divide the pastry dough into two pieces, one somewhat larger than the other. Roll out the larger piece on a floured board to a 13-inch circle. Transfer it to the pie plate, gently easing it into the bottom and up the sides of the plate. Do not trim the overhang.

For the filling, combine the sugar (adding it according to your taste and the tartness of the apples), flour, cornstarch, cinnamon, nutmeg, allspice, and salt in a large bowl and toss well. Peel and core the apples and cut them into ½ inch-thick slices. Add them to the sugar mixture along with the cranberry relish and currants. Toss the mixture with a rubber spatula until it is well mixed.

Transfer the mixture to the pastry-lined pan. Cut the butter into small bits and scatter them over the top. Roll out the smaller piece of dough to fit the top. Drape it over the pie and pinch the edges to seal them. Brush the top with the whipping cream and then sprinkle it with the sugar and cinnamon. Cut several gashes in the top crust so steam can escape. If there are leftover scraps of dough, cut out the shapes of apples or some leaves to decorate the pie, if desired. Glaze and sugar them and place them on the pie.

Line a jelly-roll pan with aluminum foil. Place the pie on the pan to catch drips. Bake until the crust is golden and the apples are tender, 55 to 60 minutes. If the edges of the crust are browning too much, cover them with foil during the last 15 minutes of baking.

Serve the pie warm with scoops of vanilla ice cream.

Key Lime Pie

Makes 1 9-inch pie
8 servings

Ever since I tasted my first one in Florida when I was eight, the flowery, intense aroma and flavor of Key lime pie have enchanted me. Unfortunately for me, for a long time it was one of those things that you could taste only in Florida, not far from the shadow of a Key lime tree.

Several years ago Key limes started showing up in the markets very sporadically. When they're around, stock up. Squeeze the juice from those you can't use and stash it in the freezer until the urge for a pie arises. Fortunately, bottled Key lime juice is available and it makes a darned good pie. Although some say that a respectable Key lime pie can be made with Persian limes (those common in the marketplace), it just isn't the same.

Up until recently, the recipe for the filling was pretty standard. But, alas, it has raw egg yolks, which some people worry about eating. This filling uses cream cheese in lieu of egg yolks, thus eliminating any potential problems.

CRUST
1 cup sweetened flaked coconut
5¼ ounces lemon cookies (I use
    Pepperidge Farm Lemon Nut Crunch
    cookies)
4 tablespoons unsalted butter, melted

FILLING
6 ounces cream cheese, softened
1 can (14 ounces) sweetened condensed
    milk
½ cup Key lime juice
1½ cups whipping cream
3 tablespoons confectioners' sugar

Heat the oven to 400°F. Spread the coconut in a 9-inch pie plate. Bake until it is golden, about 10 minutes, stirring it several times so it browns evenly. Watch closely so it does not burn—once it begins to take on color, it will toast very quickly. Remove it from the oven and let it cool slightly.

Transfer the toasted coconut to a food processor or blender along with the cookies. Process or blend until the cookies are ground into fine crumbs. Add the melted butter and mix well. Transfer the crumbs to the pie plate.

Put your hand into a plastic sandwich bag and press the crumbs evenly into the bottom and up the sides of the pie plate. Bake until the crust browns a bit, 8 to 10 minutes. Set aside to cool.

For the filling, mix the cream cheese with the condensed milk in the processor or with a mixer until smooth. Add the lime juice and mix well. Whip ½ cup of the cream until it holds soft peaks. Fold it into the lime filling. Pour the filling into the cooled crust, cover loosely, and refrigerate at least 6 hours or overnight.

At serving time, whip the remaining cream until it holds soft peaks. Add the confectioners' sugar and mix well. Spread the cream over the top of the pie. If desired, the whipped cream can be put into a pastry bag with a decorative tip and piped onto the pie. Keep the pie refrigerated until serving time.

Citrus Tart

Makes 1 8-inch round tart
6 to 8 servings

This tart tastes of tropical sunshine. It is refreshing and light, just the ticket for the end of a rich or spicy meal. Its several tart citrus flavors blend harmoniously in a most sublime filling. The crust is crunchy and flavorful, with coconut adding another tropical touch.

CRUST
1 cup sweetened flaked coconut
4 ounces shortbread cookies
1 tablespoon granulated sugar
4 tablespoons unsalted butter, melted

FILLING
⅔ cup granulated sugar
Finely grated zest of ¼ grapefruit
Finely grated zest of 1 lime
1 large whole egg
4 large egg yolks
3 tablespoons lime juice
3 tablespoons orange juice
3 tablespoons grapefruit juice
3 tablespoons whipping cream
6 tablespoons unsalted butter, softened

Heat the oven to 375°F. Butter a shallow 8-inch pie plate.

Spread the coconut on a baking sheet. Bake 8 to 10 minutes, until it is uniformly a light brown color, stirring several times and watching closely so it doesn't burn. Reserve ¼ cup for a garnish. Put the rest in a food processor with the cookies and sugar. Mix until finely ground. Add melted butter and mix well. Press the crumbs into the bottom and up the sides of the pie plate, working through a sheet of plastic wrap.

Bake until the crust is set, 12 to 15 minutes. If the sides slip down during baking, gently and carefully slip them back into place while the crust is still hot. Cool completely.

For the filling, combine the sugar, grapefruit zest, and lime zest in a medium-sized bowl. Whisk together lightly and then add the whole egg and egg yolks. Whisk until the mixture is smooth. Add the lime, orange, and grapefruit juices and the cream and whisk to combine.

To cook the filling in the microwave oven, transfer it to a glass bowl with a rounded bottom. Cook on high power until it is thick and fluffy, whisking thoroughly every 30 seconds. Cooking time will be 3 to 5 minutes. To cook on the stove, transfer the filling to a double boiler. Cook over gently simmering water until it is thick. Remove from heat. Either way, cut the softened butter into 6 pieces and whisk them in one at a time.

Transfer the filling to the cooled crust. Sprinkle the reserved coconut in a narrow circular band just inside the edge of the crust. Refrigerate until well chilled before serving.

Summer Jewels Fruit Tart

Makes 1 8″ × 11″ tart
8 servings

This glistening gem of a tart is a celebration of summer berries. Raspberries, one of the most luxurious of fruits, are suggested here, but other berries are equally appropriate, either alone or in tandem pairings.

This grand-looking affair appears to be far more complicated than it really is. Although homemade puff pastry can, of course, be used, using the frozen ready-made puff pastry is a terrific shortcut. For a festive touch, place a big white or pink flower or some gaelex leaves in one corner of the tart.

If you don't have an 8″ × 11″ rectangular tart pan with a removable bottom, you may use a 9-inch round tart pan with a removable bottom instead.

CRUST
1 sheet puff pastry (about 8 ounces)

PASTRY CREAM
3 large egg yolks
¼ cup granulated sugar
3½ tablespoons unbleached all-purpose
* flour*
1 cup whole milk, scalded
1 tablespoon unsalted butter
2 teaspoons Kirsch or Framboise
1 teaspoon Cointreau or Grand
* Marnier*
1 teaspoon pure vanilla extract

GLAZE
¼ cup granulated sugar
1 tablespoon water
1 teaspoon raspberry vinegar
1 tablespoon Kirsch or Framboise

2 generous half-pint cartons fresh
* raspberries or berries of choice*

Heat the oven to 425°F.

Roll out the pastry to fit the tart pan. Ease it into the pan and trim the edges so they are even with the sides of the pan. Cut a piece of aluminum foil so it fits into the bottom of the pastry and press it gently in place. Bake 7 to 8 minutes. Remove the foil and gently press the pastry back into place, if necessary. Prick the bottom at random with the tines of a fork. Return the pastry to the oven and continue baking until it is golden, about 10 minutes. Remove it from the oven. If the pastry has puffed up, gently press it down so it conforms to the contours of the pan. Set aside to cool.

Meanwhile, make the pastry cream. Whisk the egg yolks with the sugar in a 4-cup microwave-safe bowl or in a medium-sized saucepan. Add the flour, mix well, and then stir in the milk. Microwave on high power until thick, 2 to 3 minutes, whisking thoroughly every 45 seconds. Or cook the cream over medium heat, stirring constantly until it is thick.

Remove the cream from the heat and place the butter on top. When it melts, whisk it in along with the flavorings. Cover with plastic wrap and refrigerate until it is well chilled. (Pastry cream can be made 2 days in advance and refrigerated.) Whisk until it is smooth before using.

For the glaze, heat the sugar, water, and vinegar to a boil and then cook 1 minute, stirring so the sugar dissolves. Remove the glaze from the heat and add the Kirsch or Framboise. Set aside to cool.

To assemble the tart, pour the chilled pastry cream into the tart shell, spreading it evenly. Using a small brush, paint the exposed top edge of the crust with a small amount of the glaze.

Place the berries in a medium-sized bowl. Add about half of the remaining glaze. Toss and shake the berries very gently until they are coated with glaze. Add more glaze as necessary. There shouldn't be a lot of excess liquid. Pour the berries over the tart. Refrigerate at least 45 minutes before serving.

Caramel Pecan Tart

Makes 1 9-inch tart
8 servings

Pecans, native to America, are an often-used and much-loved ingredient in American cookery. They are abundant in the autumn and often play a prominent part in the Thanksgiving feast, usually in the form of pecan pie. This is a sophisticated version of pecan pie that has an irresistibly rich caramel in place of the more traditional corn syrup filling. A dash of maple syrup adds a subtle but unmistakable flavor.

The caramel filling is far too good to be reserved for only one recipe. By itself it is a sensational sauce for ice cream, bread pudding, or other desserts that beg for the rich taste of caramel.

1 9-inch prebaked Basic Single-Crust
Pastry tart shell (see Index)
1½ cups granulated sugar
6 tablespoons water
1 cup whipping cream
¼ cup pure maple syrup
2 large eggs
2 teaspoons pure vanilla extract or
bourbon or equal parts of each
2½ cups toasted pecan halves
Whipped cream or Caramel Whipped
Cream (see Index)

Heat the oven to 350°F.

Combine the sugar and water in a large heavy saucepan, swirling the pan so all of the sugar is moistened. Cook over high heat. After several minutes, when all of the sugar has dissolved, dip a pastry brush in water and use it to brush down any sugar crystals from the side of the pan. Continue cooking until the mixture takes on a rich caramel color, swirling the pan so it cooks evenly.

When the proper color is reached, carefully pour in the cream and maple syrup. The mixture will bubble up and let off a small pouf of steam, and some of the caramel mixture will harden. Continue to cook and stir until the caramel melts and the mixture is at a full boil. Remove the pan from the heat and set it aside to cool for 15 to 20 minutes, whisking the mixture occasionally to release some of the steam. (If you're making the caramel sauce solely for the sake of caramel sauce, the recipe ends here. Serve it warm, reheating it if it has been made in advance.) While the mixture is still hot but cool enough to touch without burning yourself, it is ready for the eggs. If it's too hot, the eggs will curdle when they are added.

Whisk the eggs in a medium-sized bowl. Add the vanilla and/or bourbon and mix well. After the caramel has cooled a bit, take a spoonful and add it to the eggs, whisking constantly as you do so. Then, whisking the remaining caramel mixture vigorously, slowly pour in the egg mixture. Add the pecans and stir so they become well coated with caramel.

Pour the filling into the prebaked shell. Bake until the filling is set, 28 to 30 minutes. Remove the tart from the oven and cool it completely before serving. Serve with whipped cream or caramel whipped cream.

6
Puddings, Custards, and a Mousse

Best Bread Pudding

Creamy Chocolate Pudding

Indian Pudding

Perfect Persimmon Pudding

Crème Brulée

Frozen Peanut Butter Cup Mousse

Flan

Best Bread Pudding

Makes 6 to 8 servings

With the renaissance of interest in comforting, old-fashioned desserts, bread pudding has catapulted right to the top, where it is likely to remain. This is a simple version that exemplifies what bread pudding is supposed to be. The rich and silky custard is generously flavored and scented with vanilla. This pudding is very good plain, and even better when served in a pool of caramel or raspberry sauce.

I usually use plain white bread, but a good cinnamon raisin bread is delicious too—even stale croissants can be put to use. Just be sure to use bread of good quality.

> 8 slices white bread, slightly stale
> 4 tablespoons unsalted butter, softened
> 1½ cups whole milk
> 1 cup half-and-half
> 1 cup granulated sugar
> 2 large whole eggs
> 3 large egg yolks
> 2 teaspoons pure vanilla extract
> Freshly grated nutmeg
> Caramel Sauce Supreme or Raspberry
>   Sauce (see Index)

Heat the oven to 400°F. Place the bread directly on the oven rack and bake, turning once, until it is dry and golden. Remove it from the oven and butter one side of each slice. Stack the bread and cut off the crusts; then cut the stack in half diagonally. Set aside. Reduce the oven temperature to 375°F.

Scald the milk, half-and-half, and ¼ cup of the sugar in a small pan or in the microwave oven.

Reserve 1 tablespoon of the remaining sugar. Place the rest in a medium-sized bowl with the eggs, egg yolks, and vanilla. Whisk until the mixture is smooth. Then, as you whisk, slowly pour the hot milk mixture into the eggs.

Arrange the bread in a 1½- to 2-quart casserole or soufflé dish, placing it in concentric circles with the pointed ends facing up. Sprinkle the reserved 1 tablespoon sugar over the top, making sure that the top edges of the bread are generously coated. Add a small amount of grated nutmeg (or use cinnamon, if you prefer). Slowly pour in the custard base.

Put the casserole into a shallow baking pan just large enough to hold it. Add water to the outer pan until it comes halfway up the sides of the casserole. Bake until the custard is just set in the center, 50 to 60 minutes, depending on what type of casserole you use. Remove the casserole from the water bath and cool it to room temperature.

To serve, cut into wedges and transfer the slices to serving plates. Add sauce as desired.

Creamy Chocolate Pudding

Makes 2¼ cups

Until I was well into my 20s, I don't think I knew that chocolate pudding could be made from scratch. To me, it was something that came out of a little box and was made late at night when the big chocolate attack came. Of course you can make it without a box. Not only is it easy, it is incredibly delicious with the most heavenly, satin-smooth texture imaginable.

As a throwback to my childhood days, I sometimes put still-warm pudding in a small dish and pour cream over the top. A little dollop of whipped cream over chilled pudding is also quite nice.

With a minor adjustment, the pudding can be used as the basis for one heck of a chocolate cream pie. Make the pudding using 3 tablespoons cornstarch instead of 2. Then simply pour the chilled pudding into the baked crust of your choice and cover it with a mountain of whipped cream. Chocolate shot or chocolate curls make a lovely garnish.

4 ounces bittersweet or semisweet
  chocolate
2 cups whole milk
2 tablespoons cornstarch
2 large egg yolks
1 large whole egg
½ cup granulated sugar
¼ cup unsweetened cocoa powder
2 tablespoons unsalted butter
1 tablespoon pure vanilla extract or
  equal parts vanilla and brandy or
  other preferred liqueur
Whipped cream for serving
Chocolate shot or chocolate curls as
  desired

Cut the chocolate into small pieces and set them aside. Put ¼ cup of the milk in a small dish. Add the cornstarch and stir until it becomes a smooth paste. Set aside. Put the egg yolks and egg in a small dish and beat them lightly with a fork, just enough to break them up. Set aside.

Whisk the remaining milk, sugar, and cocoa together in a heavy, medium-sized saucepan. Bring to a simmer over medium-high heat, whisking until the mixture is completely blended. Add the chocolate and cook gently until it has melted. Whisking constantly as you do so, add the eggs in a thin, steady stream, and then whisk in the cornstarch mixture.

Cook, whisking constantly, until the mixture thickens and large bubbles come to the surface. Remove the pudding from the heat and add the butter and vanilla and/ or liqueur. Whisk until the butter is melted and well incorporated into the chocolate.

Transfer the pudding to individual serving dishes or one large one. Cover with plastic wrap and refrigerate until well chilled. Serve with whipped cream and chocolate shot or chocolate curls as desired.

Indian Pudding

Makes 6 to 8 servings

Indian pudding is one of our oldest desserts, clearly the innovation of the early New England settlers learning to make do with the ingredients at hand. Taking a cue from the native inhabitants, they devised this creamy pudding that surely offered warmth and sustenance over the course of many a cold winter.

Traditionally, the pudding is made with molasses. The maple syrup that is used here, however, imparts a more subtle flavor that seems more in harmony with the other ingredients. If you've had Indian pudding before, you'll probably need no coaching to try this one. If you haven't yet tasted it, by all means do. It is comfort food—pure, sweet, and wonderful.

> 2½ cups whole milk
> 6 tablespoons fine yellow cornmeal
> 3½ tablespoons unsalted butter
> 2 tablespoons light brown sugar
> ½ teaspoon cinnamon
> ½ teaspoon allspice
> ¼ teaspoon freshly grated nutmeg
> ¼ teaspoon salt
> ½ cup pure maple syrup
> ¾ cup half-and-half

Heat the oven to 350°F. Butter a 2-quart casserole and have ready a shallow baking pan that will hold the casserole.

Heat the milk to just below the boil in a medium-sized saucepan. Whisking constantly as you do so, gradually add the cornmeal. Pour it so that a thin film of cornmeal covers the milk. Whisk it in and then add more. (If the cornmeal is added too quickly, it will become lumpy.) Trading the whisk for a wooden spoon, cook and stir the mixture over low heat until it thickens enough to coat the bottom of the saucepan, 8 to 10 minutes. The mixture should be textured but without lumps. If there are lumps, try to whisk them out. If whisking fails, transfer the mixture to a food processor and process with the metal blade for several seconds.

Add the butter, brown sugar, cinnamon, allspice, nutmeg, and salt to the hot mixture and stir until it is smooth. Add the maple syrup.

Transfer the mixture to the casserole. Very slowly and gently pour the half-and-half over the top of the pudding. The goal is to keep as much of it as possible from sinking into the pudding. Some will sink but much of it will stay on top. Place the casserole in the baking pan and add hot water to the outer pan until it comes about halfway up the sides of the casserole. Transfer the casserole and pan to the oven and bake for 2¼ hours. The half-and-half usually forms a bubbly brown skin. After 2¼ hours, remove the pudding from the oven and pull away the skin. Underneath, the pudding should be softly set and most of the half-and-half should have been absorbed. If not, return the pudding to the oven and continue baking 10 to 15 minutes longer.

When the pudding is done, remove it from the oven and take the casserole out of the hot water. Let it cool 15 to 20 minutes before serving. Ideally, it should be served slightly warm or at room temperature.

Perfect Persimmon Pudding

Makes 6 to 8 servings

Here, in this homey, old-fashioned steamed pudding, persimmons are flaunted to their best advantage. The pudding, mixed with warm spices and dried fruits, highlights the persimmons' flavor in a subtle way, and the topping further emphasizes the rich taste of this remarkable fruit.

The persimmons that show up in the marketplace are more apt to be in the form of the larger Chinese variety rather than the native American kind, which grow in southern Indiana, Illinois, and Missouri. Though both types may be used for this recipe, the American variety is more flavorful, and is well worth seeking out.

PUDDING
⅔ cup raisins or dried currants
2 tablespoons dark rum
2 ounces (½ cup) butter-cookie crumbs,
  (I use Pepperidge Farm Shortbread
  or Chessmen)
½ cup unbleached all-purpose flour
1½ teaspoons baking soda
½ teaspoon cinnamon
½ teaspoon salt
Freshly grated nutmeg, to taste
1 cup granulated sugar
2 large eggs
1 stick unsalted butter, softened
1¼ cups pulp from very ripe
  persimmons (see Note)
1 tablespoon lemon juice
1 cup toasted chopped pecans

WHIPPED PERSIMMON TOPPING
About ⅓ cup ripe persimmon pulp
1 cup whipping cream, chilled
3 tablespoons confectioners' sugar
1 teaspoon fresh lemon juice
1 teaspoon dark rum

Put the raisins or currants and rum in a small dish or plastic food bag. Cover and soak at least 1 hour or as long as 3 or 4 days before using them.

Butter a 6-cup pudding mold or use a Kugelhopf or bundt pan or soufflé dish of the same capacity.

Using a food processor, chop the cookies to fine crumbs with the metal blade. Add the flour, baking soda, cinnamon, salt, and nutmeg and process about 5 seconds to blend. Set this mixture aside. In the processor, mix the granulated sugar and eggs for 1 minute. Add the butter and mix another minute. Add the persimmon pulp and lemon juice and mix 5 seconds. Add the reserved flour/crumb mixture and mix it in by pulsing the processor on and off several times. Add the pecans and soaked raisins or currants and pulse these in as well.

If you don't have a processor, crush the cookie crumbs and mix them in with the flour, baking soda, cinnamon, salt, and nutmeg. Set aside. Cream the butter and sugar with an electric mixer on high speed for 2 minutes. Add the eggs, one at a time, mixing well after each addition. Add the persimmon pulp and lemon juice and mix well. Fold in the flour/crumb mixture, the pecans, and raisins or currants.

Transfer the mixture to the prepared mold. Cover tightly with aluminum foil and secure the foil in place with a rubber band or kitchen twine. It is very important that no water get inside the mold while it is cooking.

Select a kettle large enough to hold the mold and place a steamer rack in the bottom. Add several inches of water. Put the mold in place, cover the pan, and bring the water to a boil over high heat. Reduce the heat so that the water barely simmers and cook the pudding for 1 hour and 45 minutes, checking often to make sure that there is still water in the bottom of the pan. If the water gets low, add more.

Remove the pudding mold from the pan. Blot any water that has accumulated on the foil and then carefully remove the foil. Let the pudding cool for 5 to 10 minutes; then invert it onto a serving plate. Serve it hot, warm, or at room temperature—but not cold—with a dollop of topping.

To make the topping, mash the persimmon pulp with the back of a wooden spoon. If the persimmon is properly ripe, the pulp should be almost completely liquid. Set aside. Whip the cream until it holds soft peaks. Add the confectioners' sugar, lemon juice, and rum and mix well; add the persimmon pulp.

Note: To remove the pulp, working over a bowl, cut off the stem end of the persimmons. If the persimmons are properly ripe, they will be difficult to peel, so instead, scrape the pulp from the skin into the bowl.

Crème Brulée

Makes 8 servings

Crème Brulée, a supremely rich custard that is delicately flavored with vanilla, consistently captures the heart of anyone who tastes it. The real pleasure is in the contrast between the sublimely smooth custard and the crackly sugar topping.

There are two options given for the caramelized top. I urge you to try the first one, which makes a shiny, hard, crackly surface. The other, however, is easier and is the method commonly used when this dish is prepared at home.

CUSTARD
3 cups whipping cream
1 3-inch piece vanilla bean
6 large egg yolks
½ cup plus 2 tablespoons granulated
  sugar

CARAMELIZED SUGAR TOPPING
¾ cup granulated sugar
3 tablespoons water

Heat the oven to 300°F. Have ready eight 6-ounce soufflé dishes, ramekins, or custard cups and a shallow baking pan that will hold them.

Put the cream into a saucepan. Split the vanilla bean in half lengthwise and use the point of a sharp knife to scrape the seeds from the bean into the milk. Add the bean as well. Heat gently until the milk is hot but not at the boil. Remove the vanilla bean.

In a medium-sized bowl, whisk the egg yolks and sugar. Add the hot cream and stir gently. Strain the mixture through a fine strainer to remove any bits of egg. Divide the strained mixture among the baking dishes. Place them in the baking pan and add 1 inch of water to the pan. Cover the pan loosely with waxed paper and bake until the custard is just softly set in the center, 40 to 50 minutes.

Remove the baking dishes from the water, cool them slightly, and refrigerate at least 4 hours or up to 2 days.

About an hour before serving time, make the topping. Arrange the dishes of Crème Brulée conveniently near the stove. Combine the sugar and water in a small heavy pan and cook until the sugar dissolves. Brush down any sugar crystals from the side of the pan and continue cooking until the mixture turns a light-medium brown. Working carefully (the syrup is extremely hot) and quickly, spoon just enough of the syrup over each serving to cover the top, using the back of a spoon to gently spread the syrup. Return the dishes to the refrigerator until the topping is set.

Note: For a simpler topping, sift a thin layer (approximately 1 teaspoon) of brown sugar evenly over each serving. Place dishes under the broiler, watching carefully, until the sugar is melted.

Frozen Peanut Butter Cup Mousse

Makes 10 to 12 servings

One of the most beloved flavors of childhood is that marvelous mixture of peanut butter and chocolate. In fact, the duo tastes pretty darned good to people of any age. Here the combination of flavors is turned into a layered frozen chocolate mousse. Its dramatic presentation allows for it to be served after all but the most formal meals.

PEANUT BUTTER LAYER
2 cups confectioners' sugar
1¼ cups (12-ounce jar) creamy peanut
  butter
4 ounces cream cheese, softened
½ cup whipping cream
1 teaspoon pure vanilla extract

CHOCOLATE LAYER
4 ounces semisweet chocolate
4 ounces milk chocolate
1 cup whipping cream
1 teaspoon pure vanilla extract

Line a 6-cup loaf pan with aluminum foil and smooth out as many wrinkles as possible.

For the peanut butter layer, combine the confectioners' sugar, peanut butter, cream cheese, cream, and vanilla in a food processor, or in a bowl if using an electric mixer, and mix until smooth. Transfer the mixture to the prepared pan, spreading it out in an even layer. Cover the pan with a sheet of plastic wrap and freeze until solid. (See the Note at the end of the recipe for suggestions on how to layer the mousse.)

For the chocolate layer, melt both chocolates in a microwave oven stirring frequently, or in the top of a double boiler stirring until the mixture is completely smooth. Set it aside to cool to room temperature.

When the chocolate is cool, whip the cream until it holds soft peaks, and gently fold it and the vanilla into the chocolate. Pour this mixture over the frozen peanut butter base and return the pan to the freezer until the mixture is solid.

Note: The two mousses can be added to the pan in four layers instead of two. Add half of the peanut butter mousse to the pan and freeze it. Continue layering and freezing with alternate layers of chocolate and peanut butter mousse.

Or to obtain two triangles of mousse, tilt the empty foiled-lined pan on one edge so it is at a 45-degree angle. Pour in the peanut butter base. Keeping the pan tilted, place it in the freezer and prop it against something to hold it in place. When the mixture is frozen, remove the pan from the freezer and place it on a flat surface. Add the chocolate mousse and return the pan to the freezer, placing it in an upright position. Freeze until the mousse is solid.

Flan

Makes 1 flan
8 to 10 servings

A flan is a marvelously creamy dessert, exceedingly rich but not so rich that you won't be tempted to ask for seconds.

>*½ cup plus ⅓ cup granulated sugar*
>*2 large eggs*
>*5 large egg yolks*
>*1 can (14 ounces) sweetened condensed milk*
>*1 can (12 ounces) evaporated milk*
>*1 cup whole milk*
>*2 teaspoons pure vanilla extract*

Heat the oven to 350°F. Have ready a 6- to 7-cup ring mold and a shallow baking pan large enough to hold the mold.

Put ½ cup of the sugar in a small heavy saucepan. Cook over medium heat, watching constantly, until the sugar melts into a rich, caramel-brown syrup. Immediately pour the syrup into the ring mold. Holding the mold with a pot holder, tip it so the caramel spreads out in a thin layer. Set aside.

In a large bowl, thoroughly whisk the remaining ⅓ cup sugar with the whole eggs and egg yolks. Add the condensed milk, evaporated milk, whole milk, and vanilla and mix well. Pour the liquid through a fine strainer into the ring mold. Place the mold in a shallow baking pan and add water to the outer pan so that it comes halfway up the sides of the ring mold. Bake until the flan is softly set, 50 to 55 minutes.

Refrigerate at least 4 hours or up to 2 days before serving. To serve, carefully loosen the flan from the sides of the mold. Place a serving plate over the mold and quickly invert it. Remove the mold.

7
Baked Fruit Desserts

Baked Beauties

Tart Apple Crisp

Mixed Fruit Cobbler

Four Seasons Fruit Kuchen

Sugar Cream Pears

Grammin's Apricot Oatmeal Bars

Baked Beauties

Makes 4 servings

Baked apples hold a very dear spot in my heart. When my sister and I were no more than 7 and 8, we were given a toy stove. Plugged in, it emitted the faintest glimmer of heat, hardly enough to soften a stick of butter but certainly enough to make little girls feel grown up. Our first endeavor was a baked apple, a surprise treat for our father. We put a red Delicious apple in the play oven for 20 minutes or so and presented it in all its glory, warm and only ever-so-slightly soft. He good naturedly dug in and proclaimed it "perfect!"

These apples bear little resemblance to their progenitor. They are absolutely luscious and coated with a sweet, sticky, caramelly syrup. Try them plain or add a scoop of ice cream—you pick the flavor.

> *4 large Rome Beauty apples*
> *⅓ cup mixed dried fruit (I use equal*
> *parts dried currants, dried*
> *cranberries, and dried tart cherries)*
> *¼ cup toasted finely chopped walnuts*
> *6 tablespoons pure maple syrup*
> *2 tablespoons honey*
> *Finely grated zest of 1 lemon*
> *⅛ teaspoon cinnamon*
> *Pinch ground clove*
> *3 tablespoons unsalted butter, melted*
> *¼ cup finely ground cookie crumbs (I*
> *use Pepperidge Farm Bordeaux)*
> *1 tablespoon water*
> *1 tablespoon lemon juice*
> *Vanilla ice cream or custard sauce for*
> *serving*

Heat the oven to 400°F. Select a shallow baking pan that is just large enough to hold the apples. A 9-inch round or square pan usually will hold them nicely.

With a vegetable peeler, peel away about 2 rows of peel from the top of each apple so that the top third of the apple is exposed. With an apple corer or a paring knife, make a hollow cavity in the center of each apple, going about three-fourths of the way to the bottom but not all the way through.

Combine the dried fruit, nuts, 2 tablespoons of maple syrup, honey, lemon zest, cinnamon, and clove in a small mixing bowl.

Brush the peeled portion of each apple with part of the melted butter. Dip the buttered part into the crumbs, gently patting them into place. Carefully transfer the apples to the baking pan. Use a small spoon to fill the center of the apples with the fruit mixture, mounding it up over the top. Sprinkle part of the remaining crumbs over the top and then drizzle the apples with a bit of the melted butter.

In a small pan or microwave-safe dish, heat the remaining 4 tablespoons maple syrup, water, lemon juice, and any remaining butter. Pour this mixture into the bottom of the baking pan. Bake just until the apples are tender when pierced with the point of a sharp knife, about 30 minutes, depending on their size. Serve the apples warm.

Tart Apple Crisp

Makes 6 to 8 servings

Apple crisp evokes sunny autumn days, cool nights, and homey meals. It is one of the most straightforward desserts of all, plain and simple and yet delicious. A crisp is especially good served soon after it comes from the oven, while it is still warm and fragrant, and topped off with a scoop of vanilla or cinnamon ice cream.

APPLES
2 pounds tart baking apples (preferably
  a mix of several types)
3 to 4 tablespoons granulated sugar, or
  more according to taste
2 to 3 teaspoons brandy, if desired
¼ teaspoon cinnamon
Freshly grated nutmeg, to taste

TOPPING
½ cup rolled oats
½ cup unbleached all-purpose flour
¼ cup granulated sugar
¼ cup light brown sugar
¼ teaspoon cinnamon
1 stick unsalted butter, chilled

Heat the oven to 375°F. Have a 6- to 7-cup pie plate or other shallow baking dish ready.

Peel and halve the apples and remove and discard the cores. Cut the apples into ½-inch-thick slices. Toss them with the granulated sugar, brandy, cinnamon, and nutmeg. Transfer the slices to the baking dish, mounding them in the center.

For the topping, combine the oats, flour, both sugars, and the cinnamon in a medium-sized bowl or food processor. Cut the butter into small pieces. Work the butter in with a pastry blender or the metal blade until it is chopped to the size of small peas. Sprinkle the topping over the apples.

Place the baking dish on a foil-lined baking sheet to catch any drips. Bake the crisp until the top is brown and the apples are tender, 35 to 40 minutes. Serve it warm.

Mixed Fruit Cobbler

Makes 6 servings

Cobblers are so named, supposedly, because their tops look like the cobbles on an old-fashioned cobblestone street. Maybe they do, maybe they don't, but they sure do taste good!

Cobblers are also one of the easiest desserts to make. A rustic look is part of their charm, so there's no need to roll, crimp, or pinch the crust. Just lay it over the fruit and tuck it in.

Many combinations of fruit can be used, all with wonderful results. Peaches and blackberries are suggested here, but only as a means to get you started. Just about any type of berry except strawberries can be used with great results, as can apricots and tart pie cherries. In the fall, try pears and cranberries.

A scoop of ice cream over the top is sublime and so, too, is a puddle of cream.

FRUIT
3 cups sliced peaches
3 cups blackberries
5 to 6 tablespoons granulated sugar
1 tablespoon fresh lemon juice
1 tablespoon unbleached all-purpose
  flour
Generous dash cinnamon

SUGAR CREAM BISCUIT
1 cup unbleached all-purpose flour
3 tablespoons granulated sugar
2 teaspoons baking powder
⅛ teaspoon salt
5 tablespoons unsalted butter, chilled
½ cup plus 1 tablespoon whipping
  cream

Heat the oven to 400°F. Have a 2-quart casserole ready.

Toss the fruit together in the baking dish. Add the sugar (adjusting the amount depending on how sweet the fruit is), lemon juice, flour, and cinnamon and toss lightly.

For the biscuit, combine the flour, 2 tablespoons sugar, baking powder, and salt in a food processor or in a mixing bowl. Cut the butter into 6 equal pieces and add it as well. Process the ingredients with the metal blade or mix them with a pastry blender until the butter is cut to the size of small peas. Add ½ cup of the cream. Process or mix again, just until the ingredients clump together in a ball.

Transfer the mixture to a large plastic food bag. Working through the bag, shape the dough into a ball, and then flatten it into a circle slightly larger than the diameter of the casserole. Place the circle over the fruit and tuck the edges under. Brush the remaining 1 tablespoon cream over the dough and sprinkle it with the remaining 1 tablespoon sugar.

Bake until the biscuit is well browned, about 45 minutes. When you think it is ready, remove it from the oven. Insert a small pointed knife into the biscuit. It should be fully baked where the biscuit and fruit meet. If it is doughy, return it to the oven until it is done.

Serve the cobbler warm or at room temperature.

Four Seasons Fruit Kuchen

Makes 1 9-inch kuchen
6 to 8 servings

Despite their German name and German origins, kuchens are very much a part of the American dessert scene. There are many different styles, some with a cakey base, others with a pastry crust, and some, like this one, with a crumbly, buttery crust. This traditionally is an autumn dessert but it is far too good to limit it to those brief months. It can be served for dessert after a casual supper or at the conclusion of brunch. Use whatever type of fruit suits your fancy.

CRUST
1¼ cups unbleached all-purpose flour
¼ cup granulated sugar
¼ teaspoon ground ginger
¼ teaspoon salt
⅛ teaspoon ground allspice
1¼ sticks unsalted butter, chilled

FILLING
3 large egg yolks
1 cup granulated sugar
½ cup sour cream
¼ cup unbleached all-purpose flour
2 teaspoons pure vanilla extract
About 1½ pounds ripe fruit: peaches,
*   pears, plums, apricots, or apples*

Heat the oven to 400°F. You'll need an ungreased 9-inch-round by 1½-inch-deep tart pan with a removable bottom and a baking sheet to set it on.

To make the crust, combine the flour, sugar, ginger, salt, and allspice in a food processor. Cut the chilled butter into 8 pieces and add it as well. Run the machine until the butter is in small bits, about the size of peas.

If you don't have a processor, combine the dry ingredients in a bowl. Cut the butter into small pieces. Add it to the bowl and cut it in with a pastry blender or 2 forks until the butter is cut to the size of small peas.

Reserve ½ cup of the crust to be used for the topping and put it in the refrigerator. Press the rest into the bottom and up the sides of the tart pan. Place the pan on the baking sheet. Bake until the crust is lightly colored, about 20 minutes. Remove it from the oven and reduce the oven temperature to 350°F.

For the filling, whisk the egg yolks. Add the sugar and stir until the mixture is thick and light colored. Add the sour cream, flour, and vanilla.

Peel the fruit, unless you are using plums, which can be left unpeeled. Cut the fruit in half lengthwise and remove the pit or core. Place the halves, cut side down, on a board and cut them into ¼-inch slices, leaving the slices assembled in the shape of the fruit. Slip a metal spatula under the fruit slices and carefully transfer them to the crust, spacing them out equally. When all of the fruit is in place, carefully add the filling and sprinkle the reserved crumbs over the top.

Return the kuchen to the oven and bake it until the fruit is tender and the filling is set, 40 to 50 minutes. The time required will vary with the fruit chosen. Serve warm or at room temperature.

Sugar Cream Pears

Makes 6 servings

Some of the best desserts are the most simple ones, a point that is proven by this recipe in which juicy pears are combined with a bit of sugar and butter. A jot of cream further enriches the dish, and a splash of brandy adds a subtle edge.

The pears can be served with just the supremely rich pan juices spooned over them, but there may be times when the temptation to add a scoop of coffee ice cream is just too great. Give in to it.

4 ripe but firm pears
1½ tablespoons brandy
4 tablespoons granulated sugar
4 tablespoons unsalted butter
½ cup whipping cream

Heat the oven to 500°F. Have an 8- or 9-inch glass pie plate ready.

Peel the pears and cut them in half lengthwise. Remove the cores with a melon baller. Cut each half lengthwise into 4 wedges. Place the pieces in the pie plate and sprinkle the brandy and then the sugar over them. Cut the butter into small pieces and scatter them over the top.

Bake until the pears are tender, turning them over once halfway through the cooking. The pears will be done in about 18 to 22 minutes, depending on how ripe they are. Remove the pan from the oven. Pour the cream over the pears and broil them, watching closely, just until they are bubbly and lightly browned, 2 to 4 minutes. Serve them hot.

Grammin's Apricot Oatmeal Bars

Makes about 16 2-inch bars

These delicious yet easy-to-make apricot bars bring back childhood memories of savoring their intoxicating aromas in Grandma Min's kitchen. For me, these bars epitomize a simple homey dessert. I couldn't possibly leave out this old family recipe that is too good not to pass on.

> 1½ cups rolled oats
> 1½ cups unbleached all-purpose flour
> 1 cup light brown sugar
> 1 teaspoon baking powder
> ¼ teaspoon salt
> 1½ sticks unsalted butter, chilled
> 1 cup apricot preserves

Heat the oven to 375°F. Butter an 11″ × 7″ baking pan.

Combine the oats, flour, sugar, baking powder, and salt in a food processor or mixing bowl. Cut the butter into 10 pieces and mix it in with the metal blade of the processor or with a pastry blender until the butter is uniformly chopped to the size of small peas.

Transfer half of the crumb mixture to the prepared pan, and press it into an even layer. Carefully spread the preserves over the crumb layer and top the preserves with the remaining crumb mixture.

Bake until the top is golden brown, 30 to 35 minutes. Cool 20 minutes and then cut into squares. Cool the bars completely before serving them.

8
Sauces

❀◉❀

Caramel Sauce Supreme

Hot Fudge Sauce

Butterscotch Pecan Sauce

Chocolate Pouring Sauce

Fresh Blackberry Riesling Sauce

Nantucket Nancy's Sour Cream Sauce

Raspberry Sauce

Caramel Whipped Cream I

Caramel Whipped Cream II

Creamy Custard Sauce

Caramel Sauce Supreme

Makes 2 cups

Caramel has recently made great gains in popularity, and soon we may talk about caramelholics as much as we now talk about chocoholics. As a sauce, caramel is a perfect complement to many desserts, from fresh fruit and custards to cakes, tarts, pies, and certainly to ice cream. This sauce is rich and thick with a gorgeous glossy light-brown hue.

1 cup granulated sugar
¼ cup water
1 cup whipping cream
5 tablespoons unsalted butter
1 tablespoon bourbon or other liquor,
    if desired
1 teaspoon pure vanilla extract

Put the sugar in a medium-sized heavy saucepan. Pour the water over the sugar and swirl the pan so that the sugar is moistened. Cook over high heat until the sugar dissolves. Dip a pastry brush in hot water and use it to brush down any sugar crystals from the side of the pan. Continue cooking over high heat until the mixture takes on a rich amber color but doesn't smell burned. Remove the pan from the heat and carefully add the cream; the mixture will puff and steam and some of the sugar will harden. Return the pan to the high heat and cook until the mixture is smooth. Remove from the heat and add the butter, stirring until it is melted. Add the liquor and vanilla.

Serve the sauce hot. It can be refrigerated for several weeks and reheated in a microwave oven or on the stove before it is served.

Hot Fudge Sauce

Makes 1¾ cups

When I was a college student I worked at the Blackhawk, then one of Chicago's most famous restaurants. It didn't take long to figure out that as popular as their steaks, creamed spinach, and spinning salads were, the hot fudge sundaes were easily the hit of the menu. People begged for extra little cups of the deep brown/black sauce, poured it over just about any dessert, and even offered to pay me for the recipe. This is my version of that famous sauce, a recipe that is as close to perfection as it can get.

4 ounces unsweetened chocolate
1¼ cups granulated sugar
½ cup whole milk
4 tablespoons unsalted butter
2 teaspoons pure vanilla extract
1 teaspoon baking powder

Chop the chocolate into small pieces and put them in the top of a double boiler or in a 4-cup microwave-safe bowl. Add the sugar, milk, and butter. Cook over gently simmering water or microwave on medium power until the mixture is smooth. Remove it from the heat and add the vanilla and baking powder. Stir well. The sauce can be refrigerated for up to 2 weeks. Reheat it gently in the microwave oven or in a double boiler before it is served.

Butterscotch Pecan Sauce

Makes 1½ cups

This is a gooey, butter-rich sauce, amply studded with nuts. It deliciously graces just about anything it is poured over. Try it on ice cream—vanilla if you're a purist, butter pecan if you're looking for a special treat.

1 cup light brown sugar
3 tablespoons water
2 tablespoons light corn syrup
2 teaspoons fresh lemon juice
½ cup whipping cream
1 tablespoon unsalted butter
1 tablespoon dark rum, brandy, or
   bourbon
1 teaspoon pure vanilla extract
1 cup toasted coarsely chopped pecans

Combine the brown sugar, water, corn syrup, and lemon juice in a 2½-quart pan. Heat the mixture to a boil over high heat and then cook it 5 minutes. Add the cream and return it to a boil. Cook an additional 5 minutes from the time it returns to a boil. After the cream has been added, the mixture will bubble up during cooking—watch it closely so it does not boil over.

Remove the pan from the heat and add the butter, stirring until it melts. Stir in the liquor, vanilla, and pecans. The sauce can be served hot or at room temperature, though not chilled.

Chocolate Pouring Sauce

Makes 1½ cups

This smooth, creamy sauce is served at room temperature. It is rich and not overly sweet.

8 ounces semisweet or bittersweet
  chocolate
1 cup whole milk
1 teaspoon pure vanilla extract

Cut the chocolate into small pieces. Heat the milk on the stove or in the microwave oven to just below the boiling point. Remove it from the heat and add the chocolate. Stir until it is smooth, and then add the vanilla. Cool the sauce to room temperature before using it. The sauce can be refrigerated for up to 2 weeks. Bring it to room temperature before serving it.

Fresh Blackberry Riesling Sauce

Makes 1 cup

This is a lovely, dark, purple sauce that makes the best of summer berries. It is sensational over something as simple as vanilla ice cream or a fruit compote, but it is equally flattering to more elaborate preparations. It is practically de rigueur with lemon desserts. One of my favorite combinations is vanilla ice cream partnered with a dollop of lemon curd and a lavish ladleful of this sauce.

1½ cups fresh blackberries
1½ cups Johannisberg Riesling wine
½ cup granulated sugar
1 strip lemon zest, about 3 inches long
  and 1 inch wide
Scant ½ teaspoon anise seeds

Combine the berries, wine, sugar, lemon zest, and anise seeds in a medium-sized nonaluminum saucepan. Heat to a boil over high heat. Reduce the heat to medium and cook 12 minutes. Strain the berries and liquid through a fine strainer, pressing on the berries with the back of a wooden spoon to release as much juice as possible.

Refrigerate the sauce until it is well chilled before serving it.

Nantucket Nancy's Sour Cream Sauce

Makes 1 cup

I spent my 29th birthday visiting my sister on Nantucket. Her three boys awoke me with a rousing chorus of "Happy Birthday" and a call to the breakfast table where I found fresh berries, some of them foraged from the woods, topped with this simple sauce. It has since become a staple in my household.

1 cup sour cream
½ cup confectioners' sugar
1 teaspoon finely minced lemon zest
1 teaspoon fresh lemon juice
½ teaspoon pure vanilla extract

Put the sour cream in a medium-sized bowl and sift in the confectioners' sugar. Add the lemon zest, lemon juice, and vanilla and mix well. Serve the sauce well chilled.

Raspberry Sauce

Makes about 1 cup

Frozen raspberries are fine to use for this sauce, but fresh berries make the sauce taste even better. Raspberry sauce is used to good advantage with custard desserts, such as bread pudding, often in tandem with a chocolate sauce. It also goes quite nicely with rich chocolate desserts.

> *1 box (10 ounces) frozen raspberries in*
>   *light syrup*
> *3 to 4 tablespoons confectioners' sugar*
> *2 teaspoons berry liqueur, such as*
>   *Kirsch, Framboise, or Chambord*

Puree the berries with the syrup and 3 tablespoons sugar in a food processor or blender, letting the machine run at least 2 minutes. Add additional sugar if you prefer a sweeter sauce. Strain the mixture through a fine strainer to remove the seeds. Stir in the liqueur. Serve the sauce well chilled.

Caramel Whipped Cream I

Makes 1⅔ cups

Whipped cream never tasted so good. A simple caramel syrup sweetens the cream and gives a tawny color and deep flavor.

¼ cup granulated sugar
1 cup whipping cream
1 teaspoon vanilla

Put the sugar in a small saucepan. Cook over medium-high heat, watching constantly, until the sugar melts and takes on a rich caramel color. Remove the pan from the heat and carefully add the cream—the mixture will give off a pouf of steam. Return it to high heat. Cook and stir until the mixture is smooth.

Transfer the mixture to a small bowl and chill it thoroughly, at least 3 hours. When the mixture is thoroughly chilled, add the vanilla. Beat it with an electric mixer on high speed until the cream holds soft peaks.

Caramel Whipped Cream II

Makes 1⅔ cups

Although it doesn't have quite the same depth of flavor as the cream in the preceding recipe, this one is delicious—and much faster and easier to make.

1 cup whipping cream
3 tablespoons light brown sugar
2 tablespoons sour cream
1 teaspoon pure vanilla extract

Combine the cream, sugar, sour cream, and vanilla in a large bowl. Beat with an electric mixer until the mixture has thickened enough to hold soft peaks.

Creamy Custard Sauce

Makes 2 cups

This versatile sauce, which enhances many desserts, is traditionally flavored with vanilla, but other flavors can be added as the situation demands. A small amount of liquor, orange rind, spice, or coffee each lend a distinctive touch.

1½ cups whole milk
7 tablespoons granulated sugar
1 3-inch piece vanilla bean
4 large egg yolks

Put the milk and 3 tablespoons of the sugar in a medium-sized saucepan. Split the vanilla bean in half lengthwise. Using the point of a small knife, scrape the little seeds out of the vanilla bean into the milk. Add the bean as well. Heat to just below the boil.

Meanwhile, whisk the egg yolks with the remaining 4 tablespoons of sugar in a medium-sized bowl. Whisking as you do so, slowly add the hot milk to the beaten yolks. Return the mixture to the pan and cook gently, stirring constantly, until the sauce thickens enough to coat the back of a wooden spoon. Watch carefully. When the sauce is properly thickened, it is moments away from curdling. Remove the sauce from the heat. If there are little tiny curds that have just begun to form, strain the sauce through a fine strainer. If any curdling has progressed beyond that, the sauce will have to be made again, using new ingredients.

Transfer the sauce to a bowl, and cover and refrigerate it until well chilled. Remove the vanilla bean before serving the sauce.

Index